Genetic Policing

Genetic Policing
The use of DNA in criminal investigations

Robin Williams and Paul Johnson

WILLAN
PUBLISHING

Published by

Willan Publishing
Culmcott House
Mill Street, Uffculme
Cullompton, Devon
EX15 3AT, UK
Tel: +44(0)1884 840337
Fax: +44(0)1884 840251
e-mail: info@willanpublishing.co.uk
website: www.willanpublishing.co.uk

Published simultaneously in the USA and Canada by

Willan Publishing
c/o ISBS, 920 NE 58th Ave, Suite 300
Portland, Oregon 97213-3786, USA
Tel: +001(0)503 287 3093
Fax: +001(0)503 280 8832
e-mail: info@isbs.com
website: www.isbs.com

First published 2008

Hardback
ISBN 978-1-84392-205-6

Paperback
ISBN 978-1-84392-204-9

British Library Cataloguing-in-Publication Data

A catalogue record for this book is available from the British Library

Project managed by Deer Park Productions, Tavistock, Devon
Typeset by GCS, Leighton Buzzard, Bedfordshire
Printed and bound by T.J. International Ltd, Padstow, Cornwall

Contents

Acknowledgements

We are extremely grateful to the Wellcome Trust for their generous funding of the research on which this book is based (GR 067153MA). We also owe a large debt to Paul Martin who worked with us on that study, and without who's strong and expert support the project could not have happened. We are indebted to those colleagues who gave continual guidance throughout the research, who have commented on earlier versions of this work, who heard us talk about it and who influenced our thinking on many of the issues we have struggled to clarify.

Accordingly (and in alphabetical order) we want to thank: Peter Ablett, Chris Asplen, Sarah Banks, Fred Bieber, Simon Cole, Robert Dingwall, Troy Duster, Martin Evison, Jim Fraser, Keith Fryer, Robert Green, Erica Haimes, Martin Innes, Sheila Jasanoff, Alec Jeffreys, Steph Lawler, David Lazar, Michael Lynch, Peter Manson, Carole McCartney, Ben Moulton, Alice Noble, Paul Roberts, Tom Ross, Mark Rothstein, John Tierney, Helen Wallace and Brian Willan.

Finally we are grateful to all of the individuals who gave us the benefit of their experience by talking to us in the fieldwork stage of the study. We will not list their names here, but they know who they are.

Earlier versions of some of the material included in this book have been published elsewhere. In particular in the following papers and reports:

Johnson, P., Martin, P. and Williams, R. (2003) 'Genetics and forensics: a sociological history of the National DNA Database', *Science Studies*, 16 (2): 22–37.

Johnson, P. and Williams, R. (2004) 'Post-conviction DNA testing: the UK's first exoneration case?', *Science and Justice*, 4: 77–82.

Johnson, P. and Williams, R. (2004) 'DNA and crime investigation: Scotland and the "UK National DNA Database"', *Scottish Journal of Criminal Justice Studies*, 10: 71–84.

Williams, R. and Johnson, P. (2004) 'Circuits of surveillance', *Surveillance and Society*, 2 (1): 1–14.

Willliams, R. and Johnson, P. (2004) 'Wonderment and dread: representations of DNA in ethical disputes about forensic DNA databases', *New Genetics and Society*, 23: 205–22.

Williams, R. and Johnson, P. (2005) 'Inclusiveness, effectiveness and intrusiveness: issues in the developing uses of DNA profiling in support of criminal investigations', *Journal of Law, Medicine and Ethics*, 33: 454–558.

Williams, R., Johnson, P. and Martin, P. (2004) *Genetic Information and Crime Investigation*. Report to The Wellcome Trust.

Chapter 1

Introducing forensic DNA profiling and databasing

The recent incorporation of forensic DNA identification technology into the criminal justice systems of a growing number of countries has been fast and far reaching. In developing and using DNA profiling for forensic identification purposes many criminal jurisdictions across the world have followed a common trajectory: initial uses on a case-by-case basis in support of the investigation and prosecution of a small number of serious crimes (most frequently homicides and sexual assaults) have been followed by its extensive and routine deployment in support of the investigation of a wide range of crimes including property and auto crime. The recovery of biological samples from crime scenes and individual suspects, and their comparison with DNA profiles already held in police archives, has become a major feature of policing across Europe, North America and beyond. Nowhere is this more apparent than within the United Kingdom where the police forces of England and Wales, Scotland and Northern Ireland have all incorporated DNA profiling and databasing into the routine investigation of volume crime.

The National DNA Database (NDNAD) of England and Wales is an intelligence database which holds a large collection of DNA profiles obtained from the analysis of tissue samples owned by the Chief Officers of the individual forces who provided the samples. The NDNAD was established on 10 April 1995 as the first of its kind. Until 2005 the database was managed on behalf of the Association of Chief Police Officers (ACPO) by the Forensic Science Service (FSS), an executive agency of the Home Office. Following the establishment of the FSS as a Government Company (GovCo) in that year, custodianship of the database was relocated within the Home Office Forensic Science and Pathology Unit. It is expected to be transferred soon to the new National Policing Improvement Agency (although the FSS still retains operational responsibility for the database). The NDNAD currently remains the largest such 'national' database in the world (it contains the greatest number of individual profiles and also holds the largest proportion of profiles per head of the population of any criminal jurisdiction). It includes DNA profiles which have been derived from biological samples obtained from three sources: from scenes of crime, from individuals 'suspected of involvement in crime' (what have usually been designated as 'criminal justice samples' but, since 2006, have become known as 'subject samples') and from volunteers (most usually obtained by the police during a mass, or 'intelligence led', DNA screen).

Crime scene samples are collected wherever potential biological material relevant to an investigation is identified at a crime scene by police scientific support staff or by external specialist crime scene examiners. The police are empowered to collect biological samples for the construction of subject profiles from individuals under a wide variety of circumstances and from different 'categories' of individuals: samples are taken without consent from those arrested for a recordable offence and with consent from volunteers. These forms of collection are supported by a legislative framework originating in 1994 and modified several times since then. All profiles which meet minimum criteria for inclusion are loaded onto the NDNAD.

Each crime scene sample DNA profile (crime scene profile) and subject sample DNA profile newly loaded onto the NDNAD are 'speculatively searched' against all the profiles already held on the database. Such speculative searches can potentially establish links between a crime scene and subject profiles in four different ways: a new subject profile may match a pre-existing crime scene profile (which suggests that the individual sampled may have left their biological material at a previous crime scene); a new crime scene profile may match an already recorded individual subject profile (which suggests that someone already known to have been suspected of involvement in a previous crime may also have left their biological material at a newly examined crime scene); there may be a match between a new and previously loaded crime scene profile (which suggests that the same – as yet unidentified individual – may have left their biological material at both crime scenes); or there may be a match between a new subject profile and a previously held subject profile (which suggests that the same individual has been sampled twice – either because the force which took the sample was not able to check the relevant record, or because the person sampled gave a false name). In each case, if the NDNAD produces a 'hit' between a new profile and a pre-existing record, the 'DNA match' is reported (as 'intelligence') to whichever police force (or forces) supplied the original samples for analysis.

In the case of samples obtained from volunteers the use of profiles for speculative searching is limited to two alternatives for which consent may be given by donors for either or both. Volunteers are invited to consent to either: the comparison of their DNA profile to profiles obtained in the course of the investigation of a specific crime (a one-off use, after which their sample and profile are destroyed); or to the loading of their profile onto the NDNAD to be retained and routinely and speculatively searched against all current and subsequently loaded profiles. This second type of consent is currently deemed 'irrevocable' by the enabling legislation.

In addition to each of the samples and profiles described above, the police also collect DNA from serving police officers and store the derived profiles on the Police Elimination Database (PED). Following the Police (Amendment) Regulations (2002), all new police officers are required to provide such samples as a condition of their appointment, but all officers in post before the introduction of this legislation can only be invited to volunteer their samples for inclusion. Profiles derived from these samples are held on a separate database and are used to eliminate officers' DNA from a crime scene which may have been left there as the result of innocent contamination during investigation. The PED is not speculatively searched. It can be used only where an officer in an investigation has reason to believe that such contamination may have taken place.

These current lawful uses of DNA profiles for speculative searching by the police are summarised in Table 1.1.

The significance of the NDNAD for criminal investigations largely lies in its provision of automated forms of speculative searching to assist in the inclusion and exclusion of potential suspects wherever relevant biological evidence yielding DNA profiles is available. Of course the use of DNA profiling for investigative and evidential purposes does not automatically necessitate the existence of a DNA archive or database: DNA samples could be collected and used simply as corroborative evidence following the identification of a suspect. Yet the existence of the NDNAD, and its capacity to facilitate speculative searches of its archive, are now central elements in the routine use of DNA for investigative purposes.

Table 1.1 Current extent of permitted speculative searching of DNA profiles

		New DNA profiles from samples collected by the Police			
		Crime Scene	Subject	PED	Voluntary (I)*	Voluntary (II)**
Databased DNA Profiles	Crime Scene	Permitted	Permitted	Not Permitted (specified circumstances only)	Not Permitted	Permitted
	Subject	Permitted	Permitted	Not Permitted	Not Permitted	Permitted
	PED	Not Permitted (specified circumstances only)	Not Permitted	Not Permitted	Not Permitted	Not Permitted
	Voluntary	Permitted	Permitted	Not Permitted	Not Permitted	Permitted

*volunteer consents for case-specific use of DNA profile
**volunteer consents for inclusion of DNA profile on NDNAD

Recognition of the potential value of the NDNAD as an important source of forensic intelligence has led to the provision of substantial government investment in DNA profiling, as well as legislative support for extended powers of 'suspect' sampling. These two forms of support have together facilitated the very considerable expansion in the size of the NDNAD since its establishment in 1995. Tables 1.2 and 1.3, constructed from data provided in the 2005/2006 NDNAD Annual Report, show the growth in the number of subject sample profiles and crime scene sample profiles loaded onto the database since its establishment in 1995.

Each year's newly loaded subject profiles simply add to the accumulating total of such profiles held on the database (although, in line with legislation, up to the year 2001, profiles from the unconvicted should have been removed and, up to 2003, profiles from the uncharged should have been removed). Between 1995 and 2006, 3.9 million subject profiles were added to the NDNAD, and

Table 1.2 Number of subject sample profiles loaded onto the NDNAD

Year	1995/6	1996/7	1997/8	1998/9	1999/2000	2000/01	2001/2	2002/3	2003/4	2004/5	2005/6
Subject Profiles Loaded	35,668	85,354	136,248	268,146	227,180	404,494	507,099	488,411	475,138	508,663	674,737

Table 1.3 Number of crime scene sample profiles loaded onto the NDNAD

Year	1995/6	1996/7	1997/8	1998/9	1999/2000	2000/01	2001/2	2002/3	2003/4	2004/5	2005/6
Crime Scene Profiles Loaded	2,195	5,866	14,879	15,251	20,371	31,750	42,765	61,431	60,226	59,247	68,774

3.8 million of these were retained on the database as of 31 March 2006.

Between 1995 and 2006, a total of 382,746 crime scene profiles were added to the NDNAD. Unlike subject profiles, these profiles are regularly removed from the database once they have been shown to match with subject profiles. While this may be done less rigorously and less quickly than is preferred, it is done in sufficient numbers to mean that the total number of crime scene profiles on the NDNAD should include only the unmatched records of the genetic profiles of currently unidentified individuals: 121,522 of these profiles have been removed during the period in question, leaving about a quarter of a million unmatched crime scene profiles on the database as of 31 March 2006.

Approaching the NDNAD

Any effort to understand the trajectory of the technical application and operational implementation of the set of scientific innovations that constitute DNA profiling and databasing in the UK requires a dense – and sociologically sensitive – account. This account needs to attend to the interwoven series of technical, legislative and organisational changes which have underpinned this development. This is an intricate history which has been encouraged by advances in computerisation and automation which support, and are indeed engendered by, the need to incorporate the routine collection, analysis, databasing and matching of DNA profiles across the whole range of crimes investigated by the police. In this book we try to capture this complexity by outlining some of the various material, disciplinary and rhetorical resources that are brought together to make-up this socio-technical assemblage.

The most important of these resources and actions are:

- Specific bodies of disciplinary knowledge, most obviously the scientific knowledge of the form and range of genetic variation within human populations, which provide the NDNAD with its scientific base.

- The assortment of material artifacts that provide the source material for scientific analysis, including crime scene stains and tissue samples taken from criminal suspects, along with the paperwork within which the narrative of their production and subsequent preservation within a specific chain of custody is located.

- A repertoire of laboratory and computing technologies that make possible the storage and genetic analysis of bodily samples, along with methods for the representation of measured genetic variation in the form of standardised individual profiles which can be compared with one another.

- A set of very dense [dicht/beschränkt] organisational imperatives, routines and practical actions that constitute a crime investigation process within which the material artifacts are produced, and the results of scientific analysis are deployed and audited.

- A body of regulatory frameworks which sanction the construction of artifacts and their use within the criminal justice system, including specific statutes, Home Office circulars, Chief Constables' orders and judicial decisions.

This [Schappenartie] imbricated set of different knowledges, practices, and routines which together constitute the NDNAD has arisen and been developed within several distinct organisational contexts, but they are each given new inflections [Begründung] through their combination and operational redeployment in the investigation of crime. In other words, separate 'specialist areas' – such as genomic sequencing, forensic science practice, information technology, police investigatory procedures, and governmental expertise – are combined in the form of the NDNAD to effect its construction and deployment in certain ways and with specific aims. Therefore, of particular interest to us are the relations that have come to exist between certain sets of actors within this complex of elements. The interests and resources of these actors are not just passively combined, but rather rely upon and mutually reinforce each other in the course of the construction and continued development of the database and its deployment.

From our point of view it is neither desirable nor practical to see the development of this complex assemblage in terms of either the linear implementation of some over-arching ideological set of ambitions or as the outcome of a stochastic series of events. Rather, we would propose that the development of the NDNAD has been generated somewhere between these two poles: as a scientific potential which has been developed in accordance with specific state interests but which, because of its inculcation with such interests, has itself prospered and grown in other contexts. While we agree with Bereano (1992) that technologies are not value-free or neutral, and are themselves human interventions into social and political environments, it would be misleading to overstress the notion of

7

a 'governmental drive' which simply steers the development and implementation of such innovations. But nor would we wish to expunge completely the political ambitions of the state from the development of this scientific technology; it is not simply that genetic profiling 'affords' certain socio-political aims (Hutchby 2001) but that those political aims have themselves contributed to the establishment of this technology (outside, as well as within, forensic science – such as in the vast market of paternity testing).

This book aims to interrogate the mutual interaction of technologies and the social networks within which they are realised. In other words, to explore how the impact of social networks has moved DNA profiling and databasing in the UK from the 'local uncertainties' (Star 1985) of their initial deployment within a small number of serious crime investigations to the 'global certainties' of their routine use for the investigation of volume crime. It is important to understand the differing contexts in which this development has been negotiated and to discern the ways in which relevant actors have invested, and contested, the implementation of DNA forensic databasing. The NDNAD constitutes a dense transfer point for a number of knowledges and practices – across science, social policy and policing – which this book aims to unpack. Of particular importance have been foundational changes in how successive governments have comprehended and approached crime and criminal justice which have, in turn, provided a rich environment for forensic science and technology to flourish. Central to this has been the development, as we explore in the next section, of a new culture of 'crime control'. The politics of crime control or, as we prefer to term it, 'crime management', have been fundamental to changing conceptions of policing and to a 're-imagining' of police work by government during the last two decades.

The politics of 'crime management'

Several commentators have argued that a new culture of 'crime control' developed in many western societies at the end of the twentieth century (Garland 1996, 2001; Ericson and Haggerty 1997; Braithwaite 2000; Rose 2000). While there are important matters of detail that distinguish different variants of this argument, Garland characterises the general trend as this:

> The most significant development in the crime control field is not the transformation of criminal justice institutions but rather

the development, alongside these institutions, of a quite different way of regulating crime and criminals. (2001: 170)

Central to this contemporary regulation of 'crime and criminals' has been the formulation and introduction, across myriad sites and in many differing forms, of systems designed to more efficiently repress criminal conduct. This is not the development of new ways to diagnose, intervene and change the 'moral conduct' of an individual (although such intervention continues to be important within the criminal justice system), but rather the deployment of methods designed to intervene and delimit the corporeal activities of agents in their social life. In other words, this is the management of individual actions rather than of individuals *per se*. This change is characterised by Rose (1999) as a shift from a 'disciplinary society', in which individual behaviour is regulated by institutions (school, workplace, etc.) that mould dispositions and orientate self-surveillance, to a 'control society':

> Control society is one of constant and never-ending *modulation* where the modulation occurs within the flows of transaction between the forces and capacities of the human subject and the practices in which he or she participates ... Control is not centralized but dispersed; it flows through a network of open circuits that are rhizomatic and not hierarchical. In such a regime of control, as Deleuze suggests, we are not dealing with 'individuals' but with 'dividuals'; not with subjects with a unique personality that is the expression of some inner fixed quality, but with elements, capacities, potentialities. (1999: 234)

Such a description serves to define a number of general understandings which now underpin the heterogeneous collection of governmental, police and private security practices designed to maximise the actuarial techniques of crime management. These strategies are designed and deployed not on ontological understandings of 'persons' but in relation to 'activities'. Some have understood such a change to be one characterised by increased surveillance (e.g. Lyon 2001, 2003, 2006; Haggerty and Ericson 2006), while others have categorised it as an element of 'risk society' (e.g. McCartney 2006a). Certainly both risk and surveillance are central to conceptions of 'crime management' and to the now routine methods used to identify and control criminal conduct. In this sense, DNA databases can be seen as one of the many ways in which modern forms of government seek and use knowledge about their citizens in general, and 'suspect citizens' in particular (see, for example, Lyon 1991, 2001; Lyon and Zuriek 1996; Norris *et al*. 1996; Norris and Armstrong 1999; Marx 2002).

Here the collection and databasing of DNA profiles, as a method for providing seemingly robust and resilient knowledge about such citizens, are characterised as part of a bio-surveillance apparatus which records the past details of an individual's criminal conduct in an attempt to both control their present activities and detect future ones. Stenson (1993: 379 *et. seq.*) has written about the ways in which a variety of forms of surveillance embody and enhance 'specialized knowledge about crime and criminals'. And like others (e.g. Miller and Rose 1988; O'Malley 1992; Rose 1999) Stenson uses Foucault's original (1979) idea of 'governmentality' to assert that knowledge of such surveillance has effects on the self-management of those whose actions and identities are captured by its gaze. The incorporation of genetic knowledge into such techniques of surveillance is then 'only one element within a complex of programmes which address the issue of crime control' (Rose 2000: 20). As such, the contemporary crime control complex can be seen to deploy DNA databasing as part of a technologically facilitated infrastructure of intelligence gathering aimed at effective detection, crime reduction and risk management.

Few of the studies mentioned above show any interest in the specific understandings that attach to genetics as such. However, Rose (2000) has discussed the relationship between the growth of genetic knowledge and a renewed interest in the relationship between biological factors and criminal conduct. Similarly, Duster (2003) has described the ways in which the various methods for the inference of ethnicity, based on the analysis of large numbers of forensic DNA profiles easily contribute to highly contested understandings of the relationship between crime, policing and 'race' in the United States. Even if the conjectures that fuel such an interest in the 'identification, calculation and management of biological risk factors' (Duster 2003: 24) associated with crime and crime control play no part in the current design of those DNA profiling technologies that are the subject of most of this book, it is clear (at least to these writers) that the genetic information captured by these – or closely related – technologies can be used for these other purposes.

Ericson and Shearing (1986) argue that the embrace of science by policing in general arises from the recognition that any process organised around an historical inquiry will be helped by enlisting the assistance of scientific expertise in its attempt to reconstruct the past. The image of the police as technical agents of scientific rationality, rather than representatives of particular social interests, is assisted by the rhetoric of scientification in which the police acquire the latest scientific and technological aids and deploy them in – to use a currently popular expression – the war against crime. The seeming objectivity of DNA profiling then becomes recruited as another 'means by which the police effect closure and express authoritative certainty about what they know and the decisions they have taken' (Ericson and Haggerty 1997: 358). And for these authors, such rhetorical uses of science and technology are seen to support claims for the legitimacy of police actions: '[s]cience, technology and law become bound up in the constant ideological struggle of trying to make sectional interests appear general and universal, part of the "public interest"' (Ericson and Shearing 1986: 134). Informed by Geertz's observations of the technological restlessness of many modern institutions, they also describe a process of 'scientific inflation' through which police expectations about the potential utility of scientific and technological innovation are used to provide 'more and improved resources for gathering, processing and analysing' (1986:137) a widening repertoire of data relevant to crime prevention and detection.

In summary, many of the studies listed above provide valuable and interesting – but contestable – generic characterisations of the significance of science and technology, including bio-technology, for contemporary forms of social control in 'late modern societies'. However, they rarely offer any insights into the specific ways in which the epistemic authority of molecular biology provides not only a warrant for the construction of forensic DNA profiles and DNA databasing but is itself an accomplishment of these 'downstream' activities (Gieryn 1999). Instead, the materiality of DNA and DNA profiles tends to be subsumed by wider assertions about the ideological uses of science and technology, even when (as in the work of Ericson and Shearing) it is acknowledged that the police not only make use of existing scientific knowledge and technology but also stimulate innovations in their further development.

DNA profiling and due process

What makes contemporary crime management practices distinct from previous methods of regulating crime is that their uses are not exhaustively determined by their integration into a system of due legal process. In other words, they are not practices aimed at administering the legal aspects of justice. Rather, they are more generally available as generic instruments of social control and social order employing methods, modalities, or technologies to enhance the repertoire of information available to state agencies and police forces. For the police, the use of such technologies in criminal investigations may not necessarily require the establishment of reasonable cause for individualised suspicion, or be relevant to the circumstances of a particular case under investigation. Furthermore, such methods, which include police databases holding information on individuals who have previously 'come to the attention' of investigators, are often used to 'pre-detect' (Gerlach 2004: 25) suspects. And because the existence of such a record or 'intelligence' (or the initial trajectory of the detection of suspects) will not normally be revealed to lay triers of fact in courts (in order to avoid prejudicial judgments of the moral character of the accused), then such practices cannot be said to be instruments of due criminal process. In order to understand both the conceptual appeal and concrete practice of DNA databasing it is important to locate its development and growth within this changing criminal justice context in which crime management concerns have increasingly ascended.

Many of the commentaries we have discussed concerning the development of a new culture of crime management in general, and the role of DNA in particular, resonate with earlier debates about the relationship between crime control and due process. Such debates can be traced to the work of Herbert Packer (1968) who, in contrasting 'crime control' with 'due process', sought to outline the ways in which crime control initiatives inform decision making about and within the criminal justice process and police practice. Packer's distinction between crime control and due process drew attention to the relative priorities given by individuals and agencies to the achievement of different criminal justice aims. Prioritising 'crime control', he argued, led to an emphasis on speedy police investigations as well as high detection and conviction rates, fostered a dependency on police judgments and favoured processes which afforded 'minimal opportunities for challenge'. This, Packer argued, contrasted with those due process concerns which emphasise the protection of suspects through an explicit recognition of relevant rights and a reliance on formal and accountable public forms of adjudication. While the former priority emphasises the *zweckrational* managerial principles of 'value-for money' and the efficiently targeted use of scarce human and material resources (Duff 1998), the latter emphasises the *wertrational* values of impartiality, equity, transparency and integrity (Raine and Willson 1997; Martin 2003). As Packer argued of the tension between these two aspects of the criminal process:

> The two models merely afford a convenient way to talk about the operation of a process whose day-to-day functioning involves a constant series of minute adjustments between the competing demands of two value systems and whose normative future likewise involves a series of resolutions of the tensions between competing claims. (1968: PN)

It is widely asserted that Packer's original (1968) account of the difference between crime control and due process priorities is problematic when used to analyse the practical accomplishment of criminal investigations and the trajectory of criminal prosecutions (see for example Damaska 1973; King 1981; Ashworth 1998; and a series of exchanges between McConville *et al.* and their critics in Noaks *et al.* 1995). Nevertheless, his articulation of the 'complex of values' which demand 'operational efficiency' and endorse an 'administrative, almost a managerial model' (1968: 159) of policing activities has become increasingly relevant since its original formulation more than 30 years ago. Characterised by others as an 'efficiency model' of criminal justice (Duff 1998: 611) and informed by an attentiveness to instrumental values 'imported from the technological, scientific and corporate domains' (Gerlach 2004: 191), this is an especially visible element in contemporary crime management discourse and it sits comfortably within the more general organisational architecture of policing in late modern neo-liberal society. Moreover, in understanding the role of forensic uses of DNA within the changing landscape of policing, it is helpful to retain Packer's notion that the criminal justice system can be characterised as 'a constant series of minute adjustments' between such crime management practices and a concern with due process. This is essentially because, in developing and implementing DNA profiling and databasing, it has often been asserted that the usefulness of these technologies is their efficiency and effectiveness in enabling the identification of previously unknown criminal suspects by the police and, furthermore, of the adjudication of innocence or guilt in court.

This is certainly prevalent in the context of the UK where particular agencies, including the Home Office, ACPO and the Forensic Science Service, have taken a leading role in efforts to evaluate the effectiveness (and cost effectiveness) of the contribution of DNA databasing to the detection of offenders. We consider these developments more substantially later in this book, but it is worth noting here that there has been a widespread dissemination of these ideas from the UK through a range of government, professional and commercial channels; indeed the 'success' of the UK experience, as a 'world leader' in forensic DNA databasing, is often cited by those seeking the establishment or expansion of forensic DNA databases elsewhere in the EU. A recent example of this was in April 2005 when the *Garda* (Republic of Ireland Police) Commissioner, Noel Conroy, made a speech calling for the introduction of a national DNA database and cited the experience in the UK where, he claimed, the database had resulted in a 5 per cent reduction in crime and a 50 per cent increase in detections. Such statistics are highly problematic, as we discuss in Chapter 6, but are regularly deployed to argue for the significant success for crime management objectives which DNA databasing is capable of delivering.

Indeed, as Derek Beyleveld (1997) has argued, this notion of DNA databasing as a mechanism for controlling crime, has underwritten a number of arguments and justifications for expanding the reach of the technology. For instance, it has provided a platform for arguing that the police should have maximum access to DNA profiles from all individuals, that consent should not be required to collect samples, that the police should be able to retain all samples and profiles, that all obtained profiles should be available for speculative searching on a database, that no special regulation of forensic laboratories is necessary since the evidence they produce is evaluated at trial stage, and that DNA evidence is sufficient to secure conviction (Beyleveld 1997: 5–8). Variations on these arguments are made on a continual basis in the UK by those who seek an increase and extension in the reach of forensic DNA within policing. While the views listed above are ideal types – for instance, it would be rare to find even the most enthusiastic proponent of DNA arguing that the police should be able to take samples from anyone under any circumstances (i.e. with no grounds for suspicion of involvement in any illegal activity) – they are the basis for a number of adapted arguments made by a range of stakeholders. Importantly, they are representative of the central concern with using this scientific and technological resource to enhance and extend methods of crime management.

It would be misleading to suggest that those who make these arguments are not concerned with due process. Similarly, those who foreground issues of due process in debates about the uses of forensic DNA in support of criminal investigations are not necessary hostile to rigorous efforts to detect, prosecute and convict offenders. On the contrary, they often share similar views to those who emphasise crime management matters regarding the importance of detecting crime and punishing perpetrators. Most interested parties involved in the criminal justice system recognise that an effective processing of offenders which contributes to a reduction in crime is a desirable objective. However, what does differ for those who prioritise due process issues in discussions about DNA profiling and databasing are fundamental ideas about how, when and why these technologies may be used by the police. As Packer (1968) argues, the concern for due process is deeply rooted within formal structures of law and not within crime management *per se*. If crime management values stress the importance of the early effective application of DNA profiling and databasing by investigators, due process values can be seen to stress the importance of controlling the operational uses of the technology with appropriate levels of administrative or even judicial supervision. Furthermore, those concerned with due process emphasise that the importance of the technology lies in its evidential contribution to a system in which adjudication is made regarding the innocence or guilt of suspects – that is, in court and not by the police. At the heart of due process is the ideal of the 'presumption of innocence' and this ideal underwrites a number of arguments about how individuals should be treated throughout the criminal process.

Central to a due process focus is the ideal that the criminal justice system acts not to convict offenders – although that may be one of its outcomes – but to discern and adjudicate fairness. From this perspective it is the courts rather than the police who hold definitive authority for the disposition of those suspected of or charged with criminal offences. It therefore follows that while the police should be afforded relevant and legitimate powers to investigate possible offences and detect suspects, those powers must be 'balanced' with the rights of individuals as guaranteed by a civil society. Since the police are not the agents who determine the innocence or guilt of individuals their authority to impose upon or restrict civil liberties must be proportionate. The European Convention on Human Rights (ECHR) provides the basis for such liberties and each EU nation state is required to oversee its implementation. The ECHR provides a useful framework in which to situate due process concerns about the increasing power of investigators to collect, use and retain DNA samples and profiles. In the UK, as we explore later, the ECHR has been the basis for a number of assertions that powers afforded to the police to take and retain DNA from 'suspects' are disproportionate and have a negative impact on civil liberties – particularly the right to private life enshrined by Article 8 (1) of the ECHR. While such concerns are often subsumed under the umbrella term 'ethical issues', which suggests they are conceptual or philosophical problems, they actually relate to practical issues in operational policing. For instance, the creation of 'suspect databases' by the police – comprising of DNA profiles of those not convicted of a criminal offence – has become a key issue in tensions between proponents of crime control and due process.

The usefulness of thinking about 'crime management' and 'due process' is that these two distinct criminal justice imperatives allows us to comprehend how attention to each of them has framed and shaped deliberations about the permissible uses of forensic DNA profiling and databasing within the UK. From the earliest deliberations attention has been paid to the uses of DNA for the purposes of criminal detection and the arbitration of culpability. In making the first serious recommendations for forensic uses of DNA in the criminal justice system, the 1993 Royal Commission on Criminal Justice focused on both the 'diagnostic technique' of DNA and its capacity to be 'helpful in establishing innocence or guilt' (1993: 16). Since that time, the negotiation and implementation of policies for forensic uses of DNA have been influenced by both crime management and due process objectives and these have been central in shaping the operational activities which require the use of DNA by the police. However, it must be recognised that unlike other jurisdictions, the UK focus has always been heavily weighted towards crime management concerns. Unlike the USA, for example, there has been no specific officially comissioned public deliberation of the use of DNA for evidential purposes. In the UK the vast volume of debate about DNA profiling and databasing is focused on efforts to develop effective crime management and crime reduction strategies, especially in cases of 'volume crime' such as domestic burglaries and vehicle crime. Legislation which permits the police to utilise these technologies, without the need to obtain specific judicial authority or approval in individual cases, is focused on attempts to maximise detection rates. In many other states, debates continue to centre on due process issues, like the need for individualised suspicion to justify the intrusiveness of taking DNA samples from criminal suspects as well as the need for conviction to justify the retention of DNA profiles beyond the end of an investigation. In the UK, however, the emphasis has been on empowering law enforcers in order to enhance the existing practices of crime management.

DNA evidence

A central element in the successful establishment of DNA profiling and databasing within policing has been its adoption by the courts. A range of earlier studies has already focused in detail on the uses of DNA identification evidence within considerations of the role of the scientific expert and the presentation of forensic evidence in judicial proceedings (e.g. Roberts and Willmore 1993; Jones 1994; Callen 1997; Freeman and Reece 1998; Edmond 2000; Redmayne 2001). Some work has been concerned with issues of rhetoric, logic and advocacy surrounding forensic DNA profiling (e.g. Coleman and Swenson 1994; Evett and Weir 1998; Lynch 1998) and others have also focused attention on the recent 'Bayesian Turn' as a general approach to assessing the probative significance of forensic science evidence in general and DNA evidence in particular (e.g. Allen and Redmayne 1997; Foreman *et al.* 1997; Robertson and Vignaux 1997).

One group of scholars, more directly informed by several research traditions within science and technology studies, has produced especially perspicuous accounts of the ways in which the abstract knowledge system of molecular biology and its technological correlates have become implicated in the criminal justice process. A cluster of such studies (by Lynch, Jordan, Jasanoff and Fujimura) has proved particularly useful for thinking about the range of influences on, and uses of, forensic DNA profiling and databasing in the UK and elsewhere. All of these stress the ways in which the standardised procedures that make up established scientific technologies are the outcome of negotiation among a variety of innovators and users and, furthermore, that the trajectory of such innovations is marked by contestation, contingency and adaptation. A special issue of *Social Studies of Science*, published in 1998, contained a number of papers by these writers which dealt explicitly with the technology underlying the construction of DNA profiles and considered in detail the history of the forensic uses of these artefacts within the judicial system of the United States.

It is within the spirit of these latter investigations into the relationship between molecular biology, DNA technologies and forensic scientific practice in particular institutional settings that we hope to situate our own analysis of the trajectory of DNA profiling and databasing. Our aim is to reveal the practical – rather than the theoretically stipulated – course and consequences of its routine integration into criminal detection in a particular legal jurisdiction. However, unlike Jordan, Lynch and Jasanoff we are less interested in the contingencies surrounding the use of DNA evidence in criminal prosecutions and more interested in the use of DNA 'intelligence' by the police in investigations. In the following chapters we will try to show the ways in which the scientific and technological character of DNA profiling and databasing in the United Kingdom was both shaped by, and continues to shape, the legislative and policing contexts in which it has been located over the last decade or so.

The research

The issues outlined above which surround the growth in police uses of biotechnology and genetic information will be explored in the following chapters of this book. This work is the product of a study of police uses of DNA profiling and the NDNAD funded by The Wellcome Trust (GR067153MA). In the course of this study we examined a large number of policy and operational documents produced by the Home Office and individual police forces. We also collected documentary material from a number of other stakeholders including the Human Genetics Commission, the Information Commissioner, and a variety of other agencies and groups who have an interest in the state collection and use of a variety of forms of genetic information. In addition we carried out more than 60 semi-structured interviews with a range of individuals from organisations directly involved in either using, or commenting upon the use of, DNA profiling in the criminal justice system – including the police, forensic scientists, crime scene examiners, legal professionals, legislators, and those concerned with human rights issues. We draw upon this range of documentary and verbal sources as a means of elucidating the operational, legal, and policy issues that have arisen through the establishment and expanding use of DNA profiles and the NDNAD of England and Wales.

Chapter 2

The technology of social order

Introduction

The growth of modern policing is inextricably linked to the development and deployment of methods of human individuation and classification. In this regard its history is marked by 'repeated efforts to rationalise and standardise practices of identification and the systems for the storage and retrieval of the expanding documentation this generated' (Caplan and Torpey 2001: 9). These two mutually supportive aspects of police identity work have been combined in numerous permutations in the conception and construction of a variety of police archives. Since the earliest establishment of such archives in the nineteenth century, there has been constant innovation in the range and quantity of data gathered, the methods used to gather them, and the ways of utilising them in support of criminal investigations. While some of these innovations have been driven by efforts to corroborate the identity of suspects who might have previous but undeclared histories of offending, others have been more closely focused on efforts to determine the identity of absent individuals from evidence collected at crime scenes. Whichever purpose has been dominant, the result has been the proliferation of archives and an increase in their uses.

This chapter situates the recent development of DNA profiling and databasing, as methods for discerning and documenting identity, within this broader history of attempts to construct and use criminal identification methods and their associated records. In the first section we provide an historical overview of some of the varied techniques designed to capture identity in support of criminal justice by recording and comparing particular bodily features. Next we go on to explore how the aims of such activities are embedded within a number of well-established state concerns – about populations, crime, and social order – and argue that it is important to understand the relationship between identification techniques and the construction, imagination, and delimitation of the population to which they are applied. Accordingly we argue that the establishment and expansion of forensic DNA databases, like that of the National DNA Database of England and Wales, is not simply a story of the application of contemporary science and innovative technologies to established 'problems' but, rather, represents one aspect of a significant redefinition of social control practices and of the population who are constituted as legitimate subjects of – often novel – crime control techniques.

Individuation, identification and social order

The notion of the 'individual', as the basic unit of analysis and scrutiny, is a preoccupation of all contemporary political discourses on crime and, more importantly for the interests of this study, of the operational practice of criminal investigations. The practical accomplishment of accountable individuation, alongside the classification of such individuals into 'types' and 'groups', are necessary features of both defining and responding to actions seen by agents of social control as risky or threatening to social order and security.

The historical foundations of contemporary practices of individuation lie in a range of social, scientific and political developments in the nineteenth century which focused attention on a new type of urban problem and personage: the 'habitual criminal'. A vast proliferation of expert discourses and commentaries, converging in a Victorian and Edwardian preoccupation with the interrelationship between criminality, sociality and social structure, simultaneously constructed and 'diagnosed' a novel human kind. This was exemplified, but by no means limited to, the criminal man imagined by Lombroso (1876). Whether expressed through the paradigms of criminological positivism, classical liberalism, laissez-faire economics, or socialism, the figure of the habitual criminal became the nineteenth century's most important nexus for debates about crime and social control.

At the beginning of the twentieth century the debate about 'criminality' was, although rooted in different theoretical and conceptual traditions, focused on concerns about classification and separation. Leonard Darwin, writing in *The Eugenics Review*, captures the spirit of that debate perfectly:

> The philanthropist is constantly aiming at the cure or the reform of the individual, and his efforts must result in those more easily cured or reformed being separated out from those less amenable to environmental influences. In the opinion of the eugenists however, this is in fact in large measure a sorting out of those more strongly endowed with innate harmful proclivities from those having a better natural inheritance. (Darwin 1914: 205–26).

During this period, both Eugenists and liberal reformers argued that the reliable classification of the criminal population was vital for the successful intervention of the state in solving the problems of crime. What is central is the idea that problematic individuals need to be marked, sorted or separated from the rest of the population.

As many commentators have argued (see for example Caplan and Torpey 2001; Cole 2001; McCartney 2006a), the development of systems designed to document identity were originally fuelled by the growth in state practices aimed at identifying and controlling habitual criminals in particular and 'suspect' populations in general. From the earliest attempts to construct identity registers certain 'types' of criminals have been targeted for inclusion. These were individuals who already possessed a history of offending or those who were deemed likely to offend again in the future. The calculation of future offending, based on a number of ideas about recidivism, can be seen as a key factor in the formulation of inclusion regimes for police identity registers.

An early example of this can be seen in one of the first attempts to construct a criminal identity archive in the UK, the Habitual Criminals Register, which was introduced following the Habitual Criminals Act 1869 (Higgs 2001). The purpose of this register was to record individuals who were known to the police and deemed likely to reoffend in the future. Further legislative measures, contained in the Prevention of Crimes Act 1871, allowed the inclusion in the register of all offenders convicted of a crime where the sentence was incarceration of at least one month, and also introduced a novel technological resource, photography, to complement the written descriptions of individual appearance that it recorded. Prison governors were responsible for providing personal descriptions of offenders to the Commissioner of Police of the Metropolis (known as the Keeper of the Records). In 1895 the work of the Habitual Criminals Registry was taken over by the Convict Supervision Office which had been formed in 1880 as a branch of the Criminal Investigation Department of the Metropolitan police. In 1905 this office was renamed the Habitual Criminals Registry and in 1913 changed its name once more to the Criminal Record Office. From 1901 it included a fingerprint department.

The Habitual Criminals Register was constructed and operated on two central principles: first, that the archive could be used as a basis of detecting offences by providing investigators with a list of potentially relevant suspects; second, that the register could provide a method for verifying the identity of a suspect once they were subsequently detained. While long gone, the Register must be viewed as an early attempt to construct a unified national criminal archive and, as such, its principles necessarily recur in a number of contemporary forms. For example, the notification requirements outlined by the Sexual Offences Act 1997, which requires those convicted of sexual offences to be recorded on the 'sex offender register', function in much the same way: these provide the police with a permanent list of available suspects to be considered whenever a relevant offence is reported.

Ideas about both recidivism and the policing measures needed to address it have their roots in scientific understandings about the 'criminal nature' of individuals. A whole range of state initiatives, ostensibly designed to manage potentially 'dangerous subjects', has drawn upon a multiplicity of ideas about 'human nature' from both the biological and human sciences (Rose 1998). The construction of criminal archives has been founded on conceptions about both the 'types' of people they ought to include and the capacity of those included to enact particular forms of social conduct. In other words, the social policy which underwrites the formation of police archives is dependent upon conceptions about the interiority of subjects. Certain subjects become the site for identification and surveillance in archives precisely because of conceptions about their capacity to commit crime. Yet it is important to recognise that practices of identification and the construction of archives are not simply neutral 'tools' applied to certain kinds of individuals. Rather, they are themselves actively implicated within the construction of typologies of conduct. As Simon Cole (2001) argues, there was no significant notion of the recidivist offender until the nineteenth century and, therefore, conceptions about recidivism must be seen to be implicated with the development of archives themselves.

It is possible to see this same recursive tendency in the development of the NDNAD and the trajectory of its inclusion regime. As we explore in greater detail in Chapter 5, the construction and expansion of the NDNAD have proceeded through legislative changes which widen the categories of 'suspects' from which the police can take, retain and use samples. In its original formulation the NDNAD was conceived as a database that would hold the DNA profiles of the 'active criminal population'; that is, that it would document every individual who had been convicted of a recordable offence in recognition of their 'active' participation in crime. The 'active criminal' is a contemporary instantiation of the idea of the repeat, habitual or career criminal.

The growth of practices of identification has been described as the development of 'bio-politics' – the regulation, administration and surveillance of human conduct by government – of which policing is just one aspect or technique (Dean 1999). Foucault (1977) describes the gradual development and implementation of systems in the nineteenth century designed to capture individuality within webs of documentation as a means to control both individuals and populations. Within policing, and government more generally, this involved developing methods for documenting individuals in ways that could bolt a form of unique individuality to a body and, as a result, bypass any social identity elaborated by the subject itself. It involved making each individual 'a case' that could be subjected to inspection and documentation.

As Pick (1989) argues, the history of discourses on crime since the nineteenth century have largely been centred on a concern with both social and individual degeneration. Foucault's description of Jeremy Bentham's panopticon in *Discipline and Punish* (1977) is that its architecture instantiates broader attempts to intervene into reordering defective individuals as well as the social relations they reproduce. Bentham's correctionalist ideal must itself be situated, as Philips argues, in the context of fundamental changes in criminal justice which grew out of social shifts rooted in industrialisation:

[w]e can see that the changes that were implemented in police, punishment and the substance and administration of the criminal law as part of the wider process in which the governing class of Britain adjusted to the changes and problems presented by the Industrial Revolution period ... The rapid growth of large towns and cities – above all, London, but also, from the 1780s, such industrial and commercial towns as Manchester, Birmingham, Glasgow, Liverpool, Leeds – with their large concentrations of

working-class populations removed from face-to-face contact with squire and parson, posed problems for the maintenance of social order that could not be solved by the old methods of control ... To cope with these problems, the governing class had to take up, however reluctantly, the types of solution proposed by Jeremy Bentham and his utilitarian disciples; these involved moving towards a more bureaucratic and professional structure for the new urban industrial society. In the area of law and order, this move meant: in place of parish constables, police forces; in place of lay Justices, stipendiary magistrates; in place of local gaols and houses of correction, a system of penitentiary prisons, ultimately under national Home Office control. (Philips 1985: 65)

A significant element within this developing social architecture was that of the police identity archive. Implicated in these changing conceptions of criminality, morality and policing, record collections began to take shape in the mid-nineteenth century when, as Philips argues, new methods of documenting large, faceless and troublesome populations were needed. But they were less an element in diagnosing *homo criminalis* who was now both the foundation for and object of the scrutiny of the new sciences of crime (Pasquino 1991) and more a resource for documenting his increasingly problematic presence.

The practice of collecting and storing information about individuals can be seen, as Gary Marx argues, as an axiom of the development of modern, bureaucratic societies in which police work is implicated:

We see the gradual and continuing expansion, systematization and scientification of police (and more generally state and market) observation and detection. For the state beyond enhanced informing and infiltration, this involved the creation of specialized units and expanded census, improved record keeping, police registers and dossiers, identity documents (including those based on biometrics) and inspections. These forms blurred the line between direct political surveillance and in some ways a more modern and benign, or at least neutral, governance and administration. (2002: 18)

What Marx describes is a general trend, beginning in the nineteenth century, in combined attempts by the state to systematically observe and document individual citizens. Such processes are widely recognised to be pivotal in the general development of modern penal-welfare administrations and the deployment of modern strategies of social

24

control (Cohen 1985). But technologies for processing, documenting and indexing the human body have played an especially prominent role in many subsequent efforts to improve the 'means by which the police effect closure and express authoritative certainty about what they know and the decisions they have taken' (Ericson and Haggerty 1997: 358).

The criminal body

Innovations in two types of such technologies are especially important: those designed to 'know' the body and those concerned to 'control' it. A constant, although not necessary linear, trajectory of attempts to implicate the body in regimes of social control can be seen to culminate in contemporary measures designed to spatially manage populations through the use of novel forms of surveillance (for example, through the application of electronic tags to individual bodies or through the use of CCTV to watch groups). To generalise these practices into a coherent description, and to borrow a term from Michel Foucault (1977), we can understand them as trends within the broader 'political economy of bodies' common to modern societies. They are instances of practices which use the body in ways that are not necessarily medical or surgical but that are designed to render it observable and amenable to control. The modern political investment of the body, Foucault argues, 'is diffuse, rarely formulated in continuous, systematic discourse; it is often made up of bits and pieces; it implements a disparate set of tools or methods' (Foucault 1977: 26).

Foucault's analysis has been pivotal in the human science attempt to chart the modern history of the social control of the body. His work traces a fundamental change in the way that the body, particularly the criminal body, became the focus for intense political interest during the nineteenth century and forms the axis of the development of both disciplinary and governmental forms of social administration. For Foucault, the body is the nexus at which three modalities of power operate in modern society in relation to the government and administration of populations: hierarchical observation (through which the body is watched), normalising judgment (in which the actions of the body are assessed in relation to others), and examination (in which the body is subject to a range of measurements). Foucault regarded the practice of examination as the most crucial, since it involves subjecting individual bodies to regimes of expert knowledge and practices. In other words, it connects the body to political and social processes of power. One result of bodily examination, he argues, is the introduction of methods for observing, knowing, and recording 'individuality'.

The political uses of the body which Foucault describes are normative in contemporary western societies. Yet the specific ability to examine the body to individuate and record it – in other words, to render it identifiable – as a collection of mundane and routine practices across many different social sites is a recent development. For while, as Simon Cole (2001) argues, the body has a longer history in terms of the application of methods of social control – for instance, in the ways that bodies have been marked through the use of branding, tattooing or amputation – these are not necessarily practices capable of enabling unique identification. The marking of individuals to identify them as criminals – to literally incise a social identity into the flesh – may differentiate such bodies but it does not provide a method to tell one marked body from another. That specific practice, of subjecting a body to examination in order to differentiate it from all others, is founded in a range of techniques that culminate in the nineteenth century 'science' of identification.

However, the history of methods designed to make the body amenable to identification within policing is intimately bound up with parallel attempts to use the body for diagnosing criminality (Valier 1998). Many current techniques employed to tie aspects of social identity – such as name, address, biography – to embodied individuals emerged from innovations primarily concerned to use the body as a way of assessing the 'character' of the person. For instance, in the nineteenth century, physiognomy and phrenology both claimed that the outer appearance of bodies could be used as signs of 'inner' characteristics and, through the assessment of facial and other bodily features as well as the measurement of skulls, a whole typology of individuality was constructed. These uses of the body to know the 'soul' do not themselves necessarily involve unique identifiability – here the body is used merely as a surface representation of personhood which can be examined to determine the inner depth of character. Yet the story is often told of how that exemplar of twentieth century identification, fingerprinting, was founded within a eugenics tradition that employed phenotypical analysis as the basis for forms of individual and social evaluation and diagnosis. As Paul Rabinow (1996) argues, the irony of Francis Galton's pioneering work in fingerprint comparison is that its original aim was to provide a knowledge of the subjective dispositions of individuals.

While crediting Galton with the 'invention' of the techniques which now underpin fingerprinting may exaggerate the importance of his work, his contribution to this mode of individuation is significant. Galton's pioneering finger ridge analysis emerged through his numerous attempts to use the body's naturally occurring features to gain information about individuals. He had earlier experimented with the method of palm printing which he found 'did indicate something about the individual's experience and station in life' but did not 'provide a means of identification to sort individual from individual, only class from class' (Rabinow 1996: 6). In contrast, Galton discovered that finger patterns 'revealed nothing about experience [but] were indelible marks of individuality' (Rabinow 1996: 6). The crucial aspect of his work was the isolation and subsequent scientification of this aspect of the body as means of determining unique individuality. Galton's early work on these unchanging 'self-signatures' exemplifies the relationship between embodiment and identification: an aspect of the body is subject to examination, rendered into a visualised representation or written document, subjected to the assessment of relevant experts, and perhaps recorded in an archive. Such a process is typical to the documenting and analysis of all marks of individuality.

The *Register of Distinctive Marks*, first published in England in the 1870s, is an important instance of such efforts and was one which provided a framework for categorising individuals according to visibly discernable bodily features. It operated on the basis of a cross-indexed system which tied individual names to physically discernable attributes. This gave the police the ability to cross check descriptions of individuals provided by witnesses with the list of physical characteristics held in the Register. It's most important feature was that it made a resource available for the interrogation of a population of bodies rather than a list of names (see Cole 2001).

It is widely recognised that a more general and ambitious attempts to subject the human body to the systematic process of individuation and documentation can be found in the short-lived enthusiasm for 'anthropometry' in the late nineteenth century. Most closely associated with Alphonse Bertillon who devised its elaborate protocols for systematic measurement, recording and archiving, anthropometry attempted to use visible features of the body to construct an immutable record of personal identity. Such records could be archived by the police who, when presented with an individual suspect at a later date, could use the archive to determine whether or not the individual was previously known to them. Bertillon's system was an

27

attempt to close the 'gap' between embodied and social identity by providing a method for objectively verifying significant facts of the identity of a present individual. As such, it was a means of producing identifications from bodies rather than from accounts provided by speaking subjects themselves. As Sekula argues:

> For Bertllion, the mastery of the criminal body necessitated a massive campaign of *inscription*, a transformation of the body's signs into a *text*, a text that pared verbal descriptions down to a denotative shorthand, which was then linked to a numerical series. Thus Bertillon arrested the criminal body, determined its identity as a body that had *already* been defined as criminal, by means that subordinated the image – which remained necessary but insufficient – to verbal text and numerical series. (Sekula 1986: 33 emphasis in original)

This reduction of identity to a text or a series of numbers remains central to processes of police and forensic identification. Anthropometry is no longer with us – its application was short-lived and it yielded in importance to the introduction of the more effective method of fingerprinting – but the premise on which it was founded remains key to a new range of biometric methods of identification in use today that individuate, measure, record and, where necessary verify, identity.

The idea of fixing upon visual aspects or dimensions of the body and interning them within systems of recording has subsequently become a central resource for the management of individuals within modern bureaucratic societies. Until recently, for example, the written description of 'special peculiarities' in British passports was a means designed to complement photography in making individual identity visibly distinguishable. The documentation of naturally occurring and stable physical features – such as height, teeth, scars, deformities, birthmarks – continues to be used as a method for individuating and identifying human beings. The scope and deployment of such practices are myriad but their objective is common: to unbreakably tie aspects of the natural body, through examination, recording and documentation, to personal identity. A contemporary example is the analysis of the teeth of unknown corpses against previously held dental records as an attempt to establish personal identity.

The new biometrics

The recent development of a range of novel 'information technologies' to read and record identity has fundamentally altered the ways in which practices of identification are undertaken in modern societies. Using computerised technology to capture and process, what David Lyon (2003) describes as 'body data', a whole range of biometric techniques is now in routine operation across a range of social sites. While biometric technologies can be situated within the history of identification techniques described above, they differ significantly in their scope for collection and application. Fundamentally, they extend the scope for data collection by finding new aspects of the body to fix upon as well as increasing the capacity for storing such information. Incorporating a range of techniques – from voice recognition to iris scanning – these techniques reconfigure traditional conceptions of bodily identification:

> One fundamental change between the new biometrics and previous modes of reading the body is that these are physical marks that are largely invisible unless one possesses the equipment to read them. They are not marks placed upon the body (deliberately placed brands or tattoos) and nor are they distinguishing marks which are specific to an individual (such as a birth mark or scar). These are the marks of any body that can be turned into a machine readable identifier. The pre-existing body is rendered knowable by computers without a reconfiguration of the body itself. The body is 'enrolled' into biometric systems. (van der Ploeg 1999: 301)

Biometric identification seeks to make the body 'readable' as opposed to, as in biomedicine, 'knowable'. Its applications are increasingly used as methods of regulating access to a range of geographical spaces and social goods in order to include or exclude different populations or groups. One central application of biometric identification is in attempts to control the flow of individuals across national borders. Since the events of September 11th 2001, state and commercial investment in the development, testing and validation of new and updated biometric technologies has considerably increased. In the United States the Department of Homeland Security has been given a large budget for the development and implementation of biometric identifiers with a range of potential uses. In the UK, debates about the introduction of identity or 'entitlement' cards have focused attention on the potential use of iris patterns as a suitable unique identifier able to bolt the personal identity of citizens to a portable, authoritative and information-rich document capable of reliably corroborating unique identity.

The development of digital and computerised means of identification has also embraced, and extended, the more 'traditional' method of fingerprinting for identity verification. The United States, for instance, has introduced a scheme of biometric fingerprinting at its border points. Anyone arriving at the United States who does not hold a 'biometric passport', which contains a machine readable fingerprint, is required to have their fingerprint taken by a border official. The 'taking' of this fingerprint involves a scan to produce an immediate digital representation that can be stored and searched in a database. The member states of the European Union plan to introduce biometric passports containing fingerprints and an archive to support these and, therefore, such an archive will potentially contain biometric data for every citizen of the EU.

In the United Kingdom the introduction of 'Livescan' technology allows the police to obtain digital fingerprints from suspects which can be compared to records already held on the National Automated Fingerprint Identification System (NAFIS). NAFIS was introduced in 2001 and currently holds more than five million sets of fingerprints and over half a million crime scene marks. The system processes more than 100,000 sets of prints obtained at the point of arrest every month and operates 80,000 searches of the database using marks obtained from scenes of crime. The introduction of computerised searching has reduced the cumbersome process of manually inspecting paper archives to a process that takes a few minutes – although fingerprint examiners are still required to confirm, through visual inspection, a 'match' between prints. NAFIS has been constructed using the previously held paper records of individual police forces which have been digitised through scanning. However, the introduction of 'Livescan' technology allows the scan to be made directly from the body rather than from a paper and ink record. Recent legislation allows police in England and Wales to take a fingerprint scan, using portable equipment, from an individual prior to arrest where their identity cannot be established by other means. This enables the police to transmit the scan to NAFIS where it can be compared with previously held records with the objective of making an identification – a process which the police term 'live ID'.

While the construction of digital fingerprint archives combines new technology with a previously used aspect of the body, many biometric systems have produced wholly new forms of 'body data'. Iris and retina scanning are examples of how parts of the body, prior to the computerised technology designed to read them, were unavailable for use as marks of identification. In this sense, the introduction of new biometrics does not simply fasten information technologies to pre-existing methods of identification, but also opens up new horizons for capturing and documenting the body. The body is rendered readable to those who possess both the means to enrol it into a system of identification and the technology required to 'encode it'.

Such systems are now pervasive in modern societies and their use, for some commentators, constitutes a continuous and insidious form of bodily surveillance. In describing what they term a new 'surveillant assemblage', Haggerty and Ericson (2000) have argued that such biometric identification technologies are one aspect of a larger set of processes which are transforming the relationship between the human body and documentation:

> the surveillant assemblage standardizes the capture of flesh/ information flows of the body. It is not so much immediately concerned with the direct physical relocation of the human body (although this may be an ultimate consequence), but with transforming the body into pure information, such that can be rendered mobile and comparable. (2000: 613)

Haggerty and Ericson describe the 'surveillant assemblage', not as an overarching or grand scheme of panoptic observation, but as a dispersed and heterogeneous range of practices through which individuals are 'informatised' across a myriad of social sites. They stress the creation of two 'selves' in modern societies: the corporeal, embodied self and the 'data double' which comprises every piece of data that is attached to an identity (from our passport details to our supermarket loyalty cards). Haggerty and Ericson's concerns are not focused exclusively on methods of identification, but their conceptions of an informatics of identity are important. They describe a general process through which human beings can be interned into computerised systems to track both their movements and their activities. This works by making the body its own document of identity. There is no longer a need for an operator to examine and inscribe the body into a separate visual or written document. Through the use of information technology the body becomes its own text that is machine readable.

Under the skin

While new biometric technologies have been successfully integrated into a number of identification practices their uses remain limited for criminal investigators. This is explained by the utility of many biometric methods of identification to verify the identity of individuals who are present but not, as is often required in criminal investigations, to determine the identity of individuals who are absent. For instance, biometric technologies such as eye or facial recognition are redundant for the analysis of contact trace materials left at crime scenes.

It has been the development of an altogether different form of bodily analysis, DNA profiling, which has proved most important for criminal investigation. Its introduction into policing has been described as the new 'gold standard' of identification (Lynch, Lazar etc.) and the most important breakthrough in identification since fingerprinting. There are a number of facets of DNA profiling that make it especially attractive to criminal investigators. The most obvious is that, unlike all of the biometrics discussed above, DNA is a truly universal feature of all living (and dead) human beings. Unlike technologies which attempt to capture aspects of the body, DNA profiling uses the very essence of the body itself.

The use of DNA to construct documents of identity introduces a significant change in the relationship between the physical body and the resulting record of identity. A DNA profile is not constructed from an impression of the body, it is not created by measuring external bodily features, and nor is it a document of physical appearance. While all of the previous identification methods discussed above attempt to manipulate *aspects* of the body into a standardised form of information, the analysis of DNA departs from a very different premise. Fundamentally, as van der Ploeg argues:

> there is no clear point where bodily matter first *becomes* information. The 'essence' of the stuff of DNA, both the reason of it scientific isolation in the first place, and, in watered down version, its forensic significance, is precisely that it *is* information. (nd: 25 emphasis in original)

What van der Ploeg refers to as the 'watered down version' of DNA analysis is the process of DNA profiling undertaken by forensic scientists. While this process depends upon the inscription of the body into a standardised DNA profile the material from which it is constructed is itself, she argues, *already* information. The crucial difference here is that it is not simply the document of identity which counts as information (the DNA profile), but the source material from which such representations are derived. Unlike all the other practices discussed above – from anthropometry, to fingerprinting, to iris recognition – this allows investigators to capture, store and use not just the representation or documentation of the body but bodily matter. In other words, what is routinely collected by investigators is not simply impressions or measurements of the body but actual aspects of the body itself.

The collection of DNA samples by the police has caused significant debate regarding what counts as bodily information. For instance, the UK Information Commissioner, who oversees the Data Protection Act, does not recognise DNA samples, but does classify DNA profiles as information. This acknowledges the fact that a DNA profile is a socially accomplished artefact which is made for the specific purposes of recording and transmitting social information. However, while DNA samples cannot communicate information without first being rendered into such forms, the samples themselves *do* contain the information which is captured by such technologies. Furthermore, police forces around the world store these bodily samples for the purposes of subsequent analysis – something which applies to no other source material for identity documentation.

This reveals a major benefit of DNA profiling for policing: DNA samples can be collected from both the trace materials deposited at crime scenes and from individual suspects themselves. The potential to collect a 'part' of the body itself, and not simply an impression of it, from which a representation of identity can be constructed, is a significant development in criminal investigation. The durability of DNA in the body matter that can be collected – blood, hair, semen – means that investigators now have access to a powerful novel form of 'body data' at scenes of crime. These same data can be derived from samples obtained from individual suspects when they are apprehended by the police. More than any other technological development in human identification, the practice of DNA profiling makes the human body the subject of a system of standardised and repeatable techniques. It goes, as David Lyon (2001) puts it, 'under the skin' to capture the very essence of the body itself, bypassing the need to measure any external surface or to engage with the outward aspects of human corporeality.

Conclusion

The many different historical attempts to render the body knowable for the purposes of identification within policing are elements within broader governmental efforts to instigate and maintain forms of social ordering. For instance, the development and implementation of anthropometry in France must be seen in relation to conceptions of social control and the effective management of crime:

> Anthropometry was both the motive force behind the radical transformation of the traditional detective police and an effective contribution to the system of criminal justice, and it enabled the development of systems for maintaining public order against the menace of criminality. (Kaluszynski 2001: 128)

Yet, as we have argued in this chapter, it is important to understand how practices of identification are implicated in the constitution of *new* forms of social order. As van der Ploeg argues: 'We need to consider how the translation of (aspects of) our physical existence into digital code and "information", and the uses of our bodies this subsequently allows, amounts to a change on the level of ontology, instead of merely representation' (nd: 4). In other words, we need to understand how identification practices constitute changes in how we conceive of society and of the management of individuals by the state. The creation of a DNA database comprising all those who have ever been suspected of a criminal offence by the police can be seen to be fundamentally novel in the history of documenting identity, both in policing and by the state generally, because of its extensive reach into a population not previously associated with criminality. Therefore, while it is legitimate to see the use of DNA profiling and databasing by the police as a contemporary solution to an older set of problems, it must also be seen as a radically new departure in relation to state interventions in social order.

What makes the development of DNA profiling and databasing so fundamentally different is its capacity to implicate a large section of the population within a system of criminal documentation and archiving. We have described elsewhere that the attraction of DNA databasing to the police is its especially powerful resource to act as an instrument of 'reconstructive surveillance' (Williams and Johnson 2004a). By this we mean a type of surveillance which is applied following a criminal event rather than as a means to observe and scrutinise action as it happens. It is therefore not a form of surveillance designed to prevent any future action by an individual but a method for 'uncovering' the actions of the past. While this form of surveillance is common to the history of policing, as we have described above, the NDNAD offers a new way of combining those constituent elements that together form an effective archive: the standardisation and harmonisation between the collection of identity artefacts from crime scenes and individual suspects along with their storage as retrieval documents.

The ideal of an instrument of reconstructive identification that can deliver fast, accurate and permanent intelligence within policing has found continual favour with successive governments. Such an instrument promises to significantly close the 'gap' which inevitably exists between the investigation of an offence and the detection of a suspect. It does so by providing the police with a permanent 'list of suspects' that is can be subject to a form of automated interrogation. While the NDNAD operates in a manner common to all police archives – in that it stores and compares one documentary form of identity with another – its potential to implicate a wide range of bodies within a permanent form of 'bio-surveillance' is distinctly new. Every day each profile on the NDNAD is searched against newly entered crime scene and suspect profiles. Regardless of whether a match is made, the profile is subject to an automated search and therefore to a form of surveillance. In the history of criminal archiving this ability to 'speculatively' search a collection is unknown.

It is the power of this resource that has prompted governments, in the UK and elsewhere, to deliberate about which 'types' of people should be subject to inclusion in it. In the UK such deliberations have continuously driven a legislative agenda to maximise the 'pool' of suspects on the database as a means of increasing its potential effectiveness. And this has involved expanding the 'active criminal population' to include any person arrested for any recordable offence. As a result, the question of who should be included on a forensic DNA database in the UK has not been formulated in relation to traditional concepts of habitual criminality or offender recidivism. Although the notion of an 'active' criminal reiterates aspects of those previous concerns and, to some extent, relies upon them, the group now defined as the 'active suspect criminal population' implies something entirely new. It comprises a significant section of the population, almost entirely male, who have at some point in their lives been arrested for a criminal offence but are considered, in all other respects, innocent.

As a result of the widened group contained in this archive it is possible to discern a fundamental shift in conceptions of public order and the governmental management of populations. The NDNAD represents the deployment of a new, actuarial technique designed to provide surveillance over a specific section of the population not easily described as 'criminal'. What we have witnessed over the past decade is a re-conceptualisation of ideas of recidivism – specifically in relation to those who were once suspected of crimes but not necessarily convicted of them – and of the management of society more generally. Such a change has impacted upon the role of policing in society and has introduced new conceptions of social order and the management of crime.

What is also important to recognise is the pivotal role which the NDNAD has played in driving changes about the management of criminal populations in the UK. In the next chapter we explore how early uses of DNA profiling by the police, deployed on a case-by-case basis for detecting suspects of serious crimes, provided the foundations for the development of the NDNAD as an instrument of actuarial surveillance. Such an instrument has been imagined as a way of delivering 'automatic' criminal detection and it has been this vision which has underwritten two intermeshed government strategies: first, to extend the collection of DNA samples from the widest possible pool of individuals and crime scenes; second, to retain as many of those collected samples and derived profiles in the database. Yet such a strategy has required the development of DNA profiling and databasing across a number of sites – scientific, judicial, governmental, and policing – in order to integrate the use of the NDNAD into the routine work of criminal investigators. In the following chapters we explore these developments in some detail.

Chapter 3

From 'genetic fingerprint' to 'genetic profile'

Introduction

In the last chapter we described the historical and social contexts in which the human body has been rendered into various documentary forms for the purposes of establishing individual identity, especially to assist in the identification of suspects in the course of criminal investigations. Our aim was to suggest that DNA profiling is best understood as one of a number of attempts to capture individuating features of bodies as well as the traces of such bodies left at scenes of crime in order to differentiate and identify them. In this chapter we turn our attention to consider how DNA profiling has become one of the most important methods for the establishment of personal identity for investigative and juridical purposes within contemporary criminal justice systems. We consider the various ways in which the authority of genetic profiling has become widely accepted as the most robust method for inferring and testifying individual identities at all phases of the criminal justice process, and is, therefore, an invaluable support to routine and exceptional investigative and judicial (including appeal) procedures.

Beginning with a consideration of the development of 'DNA fingerprinting' in the mid-1980s, we detail the first investigative use of the technology in the now celebrated 'Pitchfork' case. We go on to consider how this and other early case-based applications of DNA profiling by the police provided the foundations from which the technology developed at a number of other sites. In particular we are concerned to detail three significant changes in the UK which have supported the growth and development of DNA profiling: first, how DNA profiling initially supplemented, and subsequently became the most prominent among, a number of existing forms of forensic human individuation; second, the way in which several different UK agencies recognised and invested in this developing scientific and technological resource (and in turn, encouraged and supported its deployment within individual police forces); and third, how the credibility of DNA evidence has been established in and through its deployment in an increasing number of criminal trials.

This chapter shows how genetic profiling became scientifically, operationally, and judicially established by being actively promoted among a network of relevant agencies as a robust technology with the promise of extensive investigative potential and formidable evidential significance. Our aim is to show how, within no more than a decade or so, a novel and complex laboratory-based practice became the world's leading method for establishing identity with recognisably substantial epistemic authority across criminal justice stakeholders. Such a development was not inevitable and has to be understood as the social accomplishment of a number of individual and collective actors centrally involved in the establishment and promotion of this novel technology.

Scientific innovation and its investigative application

The initial technology for capturing and displaying individual differences based on repeat sequences in DNA was developed by Alec Jeffreys and his colleagues at the University of Leicester. In 1984, Jeffreys and others discovered a method of differentiating genetic samples by using Restriction Fragment Length Polymorphisms (RFLP). RFLP, pioneered by Wyman and White (1980), is based on an analysis of polymorphic DNA loci that vary in their length (this length being determined by the number of repeated sequences of base pairs). Jeffreys' use of RFLP revealed these length differences between DNA fragments after cutting them by using restriction enzymes which attach to DNA at predetermined places on the genome. The cut sections were then processed through gel electrophoresis and their resulting lengths measured. His breakthrough came when analysing the human myoglobin gene and the discovery of a region of the gene made up of a 33 base pair sequence repeated many times within an intervening sequence. This 'tandem repeat' was referred to as a 'minisatellite' (it was small and thought to be surrounded by, rather being part of, any specific gene) and as hypervariable (because the number of repeats was established as varying greatly between individuals) (Jeffreys *et al.* 1985a).

A probe, consisting of this core base pair sequence, was combined with a DNA sample and annealed to a number of fragments across the genome. Thus this multilocus probe (MLP) was used to discover a number of exactly similar 'minisattelites' within one individual's total complement of DNA. It is these minisattelites – short sequences of base pairs which lie outside of genes themselves – that form the genomic material of interest for RFLP analysis. When a radioactive genetic probe was applied to DNA already stored on a nylon membrane (a blot) and then photographed, the resulting image (a series of bands of varying thickness which corresponded to the lengths of the repeated areas) was used to define the distinctive characteristics of each sample. It was these photographs that were initially referred to by Jeffreys and his colleagues as 'DNA fingerprints' when the first of its kind was developed on 15 September 1984 (Jeffreys *et al.* 1985b).[1]

These and further studies by Jeffrey's and other genetic scientists in the 1980s sought answers to several different general questions, all of which were relevant to successful forensic applications of DNA profiling. First, whether it was possible to establish unique individuality by the direct examination of genotypic features rather than by inference from observed phenotypical features. Second, whether inheritance could also be mapped in the same way – which would mean the possible replacement or supplementation of Mendelian genetics with molecular genetics. Third, whether different cells and different cell types taken from one person were genetically identical with one another. Finally, whether reliable techniques were available, or could be developed, for the extraction and analysis of DNA from the various kinds (and conditions) of biological material recovered from crime scenes. In addition, reliable answers to these questions had to satisfy both scientific and judicial standards that were sufficient to support the emerging purposes of the legal identification of individuals from biological samples, as well as the credible comparison of individual samples with biological traces discovered at scenes of crime.

Studies in the mid-1980s (e.g. Gill *et al.* 1985; Jeffreys *et al.* 1985b) established that samples taken from several different biological sources (including blood, semen, saliva, hair, dandruff, skin, vaginal and nasal secretions, sweat and urine) could contain sufficient high quality DNA to enable profiling to take place, even if not all the efforts to extract DNA from this variety of materials were uniformly effective. However, Gill *et al.* (1985) showed that DNA of high relative molecular mass could be isolated from four year old blood and semen stains to produce DNA fingerprints suitable for individual identification. Furthermore, they showed that sperm nuclei could be obtained from vaginal cellular material collected via swabs to allow the production of such DNA fingerprints. As a result of this the authors heralded the technology as a revolution in forensic biology, particularly in support of the identification of rape and sexual assault suspects.

These novel DNA methods had a number of important advantages over previous identification technologies based on the analysis of blood types: DNA is more resistant than the protein markers in blood to degradation through time or heat; DNA is found in all cells, so the amount of potentially analysable material is widened; only very small samples are required; and, perhaps most importantly, the individual variability detected by DNA analysis is much greater than that measurable by comparison of protein polymorphisms. This means there is far less chance of two people having the same set of markers and enables much larger populations of individuals to be analysed without the possibility of them having the same profile.

However, despite the significant advantages offered by genetic analysis, there remained a number of important technical limitations which restricted the potential applicability of MLP technology to a relatively small number of criminal investigations. These included:

- the need to obtain relatively large quantities of DNA to undertake analysis;
- the process was time-consuming (taking several days or, in some cases, weeks);
- it was unsuitable for use with degraded samples;
- only a limited number of genetic markers could be analysed simultaneously;
- few samples could be processed at any one time;
- the visual comparison of different charts was often difficult because of technical failures as well as the contamination of samples during laboratory processing.

Furthermore, since their formatting made the computer databasing of such charts impossible, speculative searching of large numbers was not a practical possibility. Nevertheless, the first highly prominent deployment of these innovative technologies in criminal investigations occurred only two years after Jeffreys' initial – and largely adventitious – laboratory discoveries.

First police use of DNA – the 'Pitchfork' case

The first use of this novel technology by the police was in Northamptonshire in 1986 during the investigation of the rape and murder of a 15 year old girl, Dawn Ashworth, who went missing on 31 July and was discovered dead two days later. Blood typing of semen recovered from Ashworth's body revealed identical features with semen obtained from the body of Lynda Mann who had also been raped and murdered three years previously in 1983. From Mann's body, discovered the day after her death, the recovered semen sample showed it to be from a Blood Group A secretor with a strong phosphoglucomutase (PGM) 1+ enzyme. The combination of these two features was calculated to occur in one in ten men and excluded the first chief suspect, Lynda's stepfather. Analysis of the semen revealed a high sperm count, indicative of youthfulness, and police focused their attention on 17–34 year olds in the vicinity. However, these investigations proved inconclusive until the rape and murder of Ashworth occurred three years later.

The prime suspect for the murder of Dawn Ashworth was a local man, Richard Buckland, aged 17. Arrested on 5 August 1986, Buckland confessed to Ashworth's murder. Yet two features of the case made the confession problematic: first that Buckland was not Blood Group A and this immediately ruled out a link to the semen recovered from Ashworth's body; second that, although confessing to the murder of Ashworth, he denied involvement in Mann's death. Faced with the contradiction between the blood group evidence which ruled out Buckland from a connection with the Ashworth semen sample and Buckland's own confession to this crime, the investigators turned to DNA profiling to further inform the inclusion and exclusion of potential suspects.

The story of how Alec Jeffreys' 'DNA fingerprinting' came to be used to support these efforts and to exclude Buckland from involvement in these crimes remains somewhat obscure. One version is that the suspect's father read about Jeffreys' genetic profiling technology and requested its use in the case (Britton 1998: 74). Another, and more likely, version is that the police approached Alec Jeffreys when the suspect's confession was contradicted by the blood group analysis (White 1998: 312–13). Weinberg (2003) suggests that

Police Superintendent David Baker had seen coverage of Jeffreys' technique and telephoned him to ask for his assistance in the case.

Whatever the impetus for this investigative strategy, however, it is certain that the police requested Jeffreys to extract DNA from both semen stains, recovered from the bodies of Mann and Ashworth, and compare them to a blood sample taken from Buckland. Jeffreys, along with Peter Gill from the Forensic Science Service, carried out two separate examinations of the samples, one with single locus probes, and the other with multi locus probes, to reach the same conclusions: the suspect sample did not match the crime scene semen, but the semen taken from both crime scenes matched each other. On this basis, Richard Buckland was cleared of charges on 21 November 1986, and it seems likely that Jeffreys' comment at the time – that Buckland would probably have been convicted in the absence of this new evidence – was correct. In the event, the exoneration of Richard Buckland was the outcome of the first use of DNA profiling in the criminal justice system and it remains an important event in the history of the forensic use of DNA. The emphasis on this technology to provide a robust and objective mechanism to exclude suspects or to prove innocence, as well as to inculpate suspects or to prove guilt, remains central to the arguments presented in favour of its use by its proponents, and often finds sympathy among those who are less wholehearted in their support of the expanding powers of the police to collect biological material from a widening range of individuals.

Following Buckland's exoneration, and fuelled with enthusiasm for a novel technology, the police subsequently began a mass DNA screening in January 1987. The screen was organised to capture DNA from every local male aged between 16 and 34 from the villages surrounding the crime scenes, however there were a number of practical problems with the organisation of this effort which hindered the successful identification of a suspect. Canter (1995: 20) describes the screening as 'indiscriminate' and argues that sampling large numbers of individuals made it difficult to keep a check on identities. Furthermore (and in support of his own area of expertise), he argues that the failure of the police to use behavioural analysis in this case meant that they missed the opportunity to narrow the range of possible suspects targeted for DNA profiling. Nevertheless, by April 1987 the police had taken 4,000 samples of blood, obtained using subcontracted doctors, and the FSS had carried out DNA profiling on all those blood samples. The mass screening continued and, in the absence of matches with the profiles obtained from crime scene samples, proved inconclusive.

On 27 January 1987 the police had collected a blood sample from an Ian Kelly who gave his identity as Colin Pitchfork (Kelly used Pitchfork's driving licence and passport – the latter substituted with a photo of Kelly), and the DNA extracted from this sample had, like all others, failed to match the crime scene sample. On 1 August 1987, in a conversation in a pub between Ian Kelly and workmates of Colin Pitchfork, Kelly discussed how he had posed as Pitchfork in the mass screening. One of those present at this conversation (a relative of a policeman) telephoned the police – six weeks later – and reported this. Ian Kelly was arrested on 19 September 1987 and charged with conspiracy to pervert the course of justice. Pitchfork was himself arrested on the same day and admitted to committing the offences under investigation. Subsequent profiling of his DNA produced a conclusive match with the semen recovered from both bodies. Pitchfork was convicted and sentenced on 22 January 1988.

The detection and identification of Colin Pitchfork was a defining moment in the use of DNA profiling and its capacity to provide a link between an individual and a crime scene. Yet it is clear that, despite its enthusiastic use in the form of a large mass screening exercise, its results were far from straightforward. While the scientific validity of this technology was accepted almost without question there were those who raised questions about its investigative value. One example of this was the question of whether Buckland should have been excluded from suspicion on the basis of no forensic match having been obtained. For instance, Britton (1998, 2001) (who claims involvement in the case because of his work in a mental hospital close to the Mann attack where Buckland was also employed, his subsequent work with Leicester police in profiling the suspect, and his claims to have listened to interview tapes with Buckland) argues that Buckland must have either seen the offence or come into contact with the body. Buckland had, during the police investigation, revealed details of Ashworth's body which Britton claims he was incapable of knowing without being present.

Britton also raises a number of questions about the collection of semen from the murdered bodies: for instance, were samples taken from both orifices of Ashworth after she was raped anally as well as vaginally? Because Mann was, in contrast, raped only vaginally, Britton asks is there a possibility that Buckland was responsible for a post-mortem anal rape after Pitchfork had left the scene of Ashworth's murder? A failure to collect an anal swab from the body would have also failed to produce an initial blood group link between the scene and Buckland, if such a link existed, and further ruled out a DNA match. According to Britton one of the senior police officers on the case was discouraged by the way in which the DNA evidence forced the exoneration of Buckland. Baker, Britton reports, said of Jeffreys: 'he does a test that we've never heard of and comes back and says "you've got the wrong guy". You can't challenge it. How can you challenge brand-new science? Nobody else in the bloody world knows anything about it' (1998: 74).

While these questions are not relevant to the proven guilt of Pitchfork, the case does highlight many of the practical investigative details which arise from the use of DNA within policing and which have endured until the present time. The investigation raised questions about the viability of the use of this technology by the police in terms of:

- the value of DNA evidence in relation to other evidence types;
- the collection issues raised by the extraction of samples from crime scenes and individuals;
- the problems of mass screening.

Indeed, the central feature of the case – Pitchfork's initial evasion from the mass screen – is an example of an important feature of the practical uses of DNA profiling which still causes concern for investigators: the problem of linking genetic profiles to separately established and validated personal identities.

One further feature of the Pitchfork case is worthy of note: Pitchfork pleaded guilty to the two offences with which he was charged and so was convicted and sentenced without a formal trial. This meant that the DNA evidence in this case was neither presented to assist his prosecution, nor relevant experts tested in the adversarial process of the courtroom. Nevertheless, the scientific success and the investigative potential of the technique invented by Jeffreys were quickly embraced by law enforcement agencies across the globe, and the first UK criminal trial in which such evidence was used was the case of Robert Melias who was convicted of rape in Bristol in October 1987.[2] In this case a DNA profile obtained from crime scene samples successfully matched Melias' own DNA (obtained from a consensual blood sample given to the police) and the match was presented in court at a match probability ratio of one in four million. Melias was found guilty and sentenced to eight years in prison (Phillips 1988).

UK government investment in research and development

The 'Pitchfork' case was the first of several early instances in which DNA profiling played a major role in police investigations. It was itself a landmark case and also the precursor to a rapidly expanding case load that was being handled by the Forensic Science Service (FSS) at that time. By 1987 the Biology Division of the Central Research and Support Establishment (CRSE) of the Home Office Forensic Science Service, a group concerned mainly with serious offences against persons (such as cases of rape, wounding and murder), was carrying out a major DNA initiative with a remit to consider three principle issues: how to assure the rapid adoption of DNA profiling, under controlled conditions, into case work analysis; how to provide training to operational staff in order to ensure that such casework could be met; and finally, how to make research and development of DNA profiling a priority. In 1987 the division focused its whole attention on DNA profiling and by the beginning of 1988 its work was dominated with DNA submissions from the police forces of England and Wales. By July 1988, 200 cases had been received by the division and DNA profiling was recognised to be of central importance to FSS activity. These early applications of, and research developments in, DNA profiling showed the successful combination of highly specialised scientific techniques within innovative forms of police investigations.

At the same time, there were further advances in the laboratory technology for measuring and recording the presence of differences between individuals at common locations on the human genome. Single Locus Probes (SLPs) quickly began to replace MLPs in the early 1990s. The first versions of these examined four loci and were sufficiently sensitive to allow forensic scientists to be able to interpret some of the results obtained from mixed biological samples. Such samples are especially common in cases of sexual crime where biological material from both victim and offender is often impossible to differentiate visually and so is processed together.

Despite a small number of cases in which technological or techno-interpretative issues resulted in prosecution failures or successful appeals involving the use of DNA evidence (e.g. R *v* Borham 1992; R *v* Dean 1994; R *v* Gordon 1995), proponents of DNA profiling successfully – and speedily – established its status as an authoritative investigative tool and an increasingly credible prosecutorial resource. The commitment of the Home Office to fund research into DNA profiling, by directing the FSS to develop adequate systems for effective DNA casework in support of police investigations, was both central to the initial success of the technology and also a deliberate strategy to further its potential use. Yet to achieve this, the Home Office had to acquire the technology from the original patent owners, The Lister Institute of Preventive Medicine, which had previously granted an exclusive licence to ICI for the commercialisation of the technology. By appropriating the technology through Crown Privilege the Home Office avoided the financial burden of using an external body to undertake, what was then, costly casework analysis and also facilitated the growth of their own laboratory facilities in an economical way. The issue of patent was solved by the introduction of Polymerase Chain Reaction (PCR) technology which was free from the restrictions of corporate property rights.

PCR technology offers the amplification of discrete sections of DNA to allow profiling of much smaller crime scene samples. In spring 1983, Kerry Mullis had already envisaged the possibility of amplifying small amounts of cut sections of DNA to the larger quantities otherwise required for analysis. Following laboratory work during 1983, an early version of the technique had been developed by Mullis in the Cetus laboratories while Ehrich and Blake further developed the forensic use of PCR in the 1980s, the latter being the first biochemist to present PCR results in a case of rape.

PCR amplification is achieved by the use of an enzyme – Taq DNA Polymerase – which binds to 'unzipped' DNA strands separated by being heated in solution. Taq DNA Polymerase, itself immune to the effects of such high temperatures, speeds up the chemical reactions in which thermal cyclers are used to create copies of small sections of DNA very quickly. Since the replication process is exponential, unlimited numbers of copies can be made: five cycles will produce 256 copies, six will produce 65,536 copies, 20 will yield a million copies.

The development and acceptance of PCR technology in turn facilitated the development of a new method for individuating genetic samples: Short Tandem Repeats (STRs). Where the minisatellites or VNTRs that formed the target for MLP and SLP technologies were between nine and 50 base pairs, Short Tandem Repeats or microsatellites consist of between two and seven base pairs, and sequences of these base pairs repeats vary in length between 100 and 400 base pairs. The amount of variation within these parameters is large, and it is easier for several such loci to be amplified and measured within a single 'multiplex' test. The first such commercially available test in the UK, introduced by Applied Biosystems in 1994 and known as 'First

Generation Multiplex', amplified four STRs. A 'Second Generation Multiplex' (SGM®) test, measuring six STR markers, was introduced in 1995, and in 1999, SGM® was further developed to include an additional four loci, making ten in all and renamed SGM Plus®. All the loci sampled by these tests are on different autosomes, and this variation of origin underlies the assertion that the alleles found on each locus are independent of one another – in other words that the inheritance of a specific genotype on one locus is not affected by the inheritance of another genotype on another locus.

Each STR has two alleles (one from each donating parent) and so a genetic profile based on SGM Plus® is made up of 20 numerical markers in addition to the sex marker. At the time of writing this remains the workhorse test used for the routine examination of crime scene stains, the analysis of samples taken from known suspects and the source of all the genetic profiles stored on the NDNAD. Both SGM® and SGM Plus® tests also include the analyis of a sex marker – amelogenin. The amelogenin gene codes for a specific protein and is located on both X and Y chromosomes, but amplification of a section of the gene produces different lengths from each chromosome type. Thus the sex of the sample donor can easily be determined.

DNA and UK forensic science

These early applications of, and research developments in, DNA profiling involved the successful combination of highly specialised scientific techniques within innovative police investigations. But an important element in the story of the success of this new technology of criminal detection was a matter of timing. In particular that it became available, and increasingly used, at a time when the UK forensic science community, and the investigations and prosecutions supported by members of that community, were subject to high levels of public criticism supplemented by a degree of judicial concern.

The reputation of forensic science in England and Wales had reached a low point by the early 1990s, although the events which had triggered this condition had occurred during the preceding decade. In particular, seven significant miscarriages of justice, involving successful appeals against convictions for terrorism and serious offences against the person concerned, had been dealt with by the Court of Appeal: John Preece; 'The Birmingham Six'; 'The Maguire Seven'; 'The Guilford Four'; Stefan Kiszko; Judith Ward; 'The Tottenham Three'. It was against this background, and in particular the case of The Birmingham Six, that the government announced the establishment of a Royal Commission on Criminal Justice in 1991. The Commission's remit was to undertake an extensive examination of the criminal justice system from the point at which an individual is arrested, through the investigative process and the collection of evidence, to the prosecution of an individual in court. The remit was wide and the subsequent recommendations were far reaching.

In fact, the report by the Royal Commission on Criminal Justice (1993) was preceded by the House of Lords' Select Committee on Science and Technology report, *Forensic Science* (1993), which had already examined the current arrangements for the provision of forensic science in England and Wales. The Select Committee wanted to establish the 'true picture' of forensic science and deal with the 'image problem' which they argued depicted the forensic scientist as 'a policeman in a white coat' (1993: 14–15). The Select Committee defended the expertise and impartiality of forensic scientists across the country, arguing that in the seven cases mentioned above only three had involved scientific evidence and that even here the fault lay in the use of practices that had already been replaced. Their main finding was that the quality of service provision of forensic science in the England and Wales was high and they urged public confidence in it.

As part of the Select Committee's consideration of forensic science they briefly examined DNA profiling and posed four key questions. First, whether the courts do, and should, accept the validity of such novel scientific evidence? Second, how do statements of probability derived from DNA relate to the traditional concept of 'reasonable doubt' in judgments of innocence and guilt in criminal cases? Third, what are the circumstances under which bodily samples should be taken and retained by the police? Finally, under what circumstances may a DNA profile be retained in either an 'identified' or 'anonymous' form on a computerised database and who should have access to it?

The first two of these questions resonate with a large number of subsequent academic studies of the legal and technical issues that surround the presentation and evaluation of forensic evidence in judicial proceedings and the relationship between scientific expertise and judicial decision making (see, for example, Roberts and Willmore 1993; Jones 1994; Callen 1997; Freeman and Reece 1998; Edmond 2000; Redmayne 2001), the probative significance of forensic science evidence in general (see, for example, Allen and Redmayne 1997; Foreman *et al.* 1997; Robertson and Vignaux 1997), and issues surrounding the presentation and evaluation of DNA evidence in particular (see, for example, Coleman and Swenson 1994; Thompson 1997; Evett and Weir 1998; Lynch 1998).

What these and other studies remind us is that the judicial acceptance of forensic DNA technology was not simply secured by scientific authority or by legal fiat, but rather by organisational responses to legal challenges which 'spurred the formation of new testing methods and agencies, as well as the standardization of commonly used tests' (Jasanoff 2001b: 13620). Scientific technologies become embedded in legal proceedings through the negotiation and adaptation of their innovators and users, and this is well illustrated by the contestation and contingency surrounding the early use of DNA evidence in criminal case work. However, these contests were more muted in the UK than in the USA, and by 1988 the success of several prosecutions in which DNA evidence was presented had shown that, despite challenges to the interpretation of DNA profiling by defence counsel, judicial responses were sufficiently positive for the FSS to claim that 'the technique itself seems to have been accepted' (Home Office 1988: 9).

As a corollorary to that acceptance, the courts of England and Wales (like those of all other jurisdictions) have imposed increasingly rigorous standards on those seeking to invoke DNA evidence in support of criminal prosecutions. These standards include requirements concerning the collection of biological material from crime scenes, its safe conduct to relevant laboratories, control of the contamination of samples, and methods to secure the reliability of profile analysis and comparison. Since any or all of these, as elements in what Lynch has called the 'administrative envelope' in which all such forensic technologies are delivered to investigators and to adjudicators, can become the subject of intense scrutiny in the adversarial setting of a courtroom, all stages of this process require attention to issues of procedural and substantive adequacy as well as accurate documentation.

Population genetics, random match probabilities and 'likelihood ratios'

While the acceptance of expert DNA evidence by the judges in the courts of England and Wales was fairly rapid (largely because solutions to actual and potential problems were easily found in prior and current practices for the application of accepted forensic science principles and the validation of forensic laboratory results), some features of its use generated difficulties for both experts and the courts. Although most of these have largely been resolved at the time of writing, there remain certain problems in the presentation of DNA evidence that continue to interest forensic scientists, lawyers and statisticians. The remainder of this section considers these problems, they ways in which they initially arose, and the early solutions arrived at.

Population genetics

As described earlier, forensic genetic profiles are constructed from the measurement of differences between individuals found at a number of common but arguably independent loci on the human genome. Each individual person's particular genotype at each locus – made up of two alleles – is one of a variable number of such genotypes known to exist in the wider population at large. While the number of individuals whose measurement is included in currently available population figures remains relatively low, and thus the knowledge of the full range of allele variation remains somewhat limited, the increasing number of profiles submitted to forensic databases seem only likely to increase the total range of known alleles. Mainstream forensic science journals continuously publish new data from national and local collections. The current published range of alleles known to exist for the loci measured by the Applied Biosystems SGM Plus® test ranges from 9 to 43.

Once the frequency of specific alleles is known, the Hardy-Weinberg Principle can be used to calculate how frequent is any particular genotype within a given population. Consider a specific STR locus with only two alleles A and B with frequency of occurrence of a and b. According to the principle, the frequency of the genotypes will be $(a+b)^2 = a^2 + 2ab + b^2$. In this equation, a^2 is the frequency of the homozygous genotype AA, b^2 is the frequency of the homozygous genotype BB, and 2ab is the frequency of the heterozygous genotype AB. The subsequent estimation of the frequency of occurrence of an entire profile within a given population is arrived at by simply multiplying together the genotype frequencies for each locus that contributes to the profile.

There is a small genetics literature which has focused on the underlying assumptions of the Hardy-Weinberg Principle and the extent to which these assumptions can be relied on in all circumstances. Most important of these is the assumption that mating occurs at random in the global population from which individuals are drawn and the further assumption that this population is relatively large. The first of these is easily shown to be unreliable since there are high levels of within-group mating among relatively distinct geographic, class or cultural groups within particular societies. The result of this is that allele frequencies are not uniform among such groups – distinctive sub-population frequencies exist, yet at the same time the process of assigning individuals to particular groups for this purposes remains a highly contestable one.

In addition, familial relationships mean that close kin share alleles on one or more loci much more often than unrelated individuals. The degree of sharing varies according to the precise nature of the relationship, as well as according to the particular population from which individuals come. While it is impossible to automatically differentiate random matching from relational matching, Greeley *et al.* (2006: 252) provide a rough summary of the expected degree of commonality as follows: 'First degree relatives share, on average, about fifty percent of each other's DNA variants ... These are genetic parents, siblings and children. Second degree relatives – uncles or aunts and nephews or nieces, grandparents and grandchildren, half-brothers and half-sisters – share one-quarter ... third degree relatives (first cousins, great-grandparents and great-grandchildren among others) share one-eighth'. Such commonalities have been both a problem and a resource for those using genetic information to investigate and prosecute crime. On the one hand they may be used to support a defence claim that a close relative of an accused person may be the true perpetrator (especially where only partial profiles are available for comparison), while on the other hand there are many occasions on which a partial match between a crime scene stain and a databased profile may be used to infer that a relative of the databased subject may be the origin of the biological material in question.

Match Probability Calculations

Once the frequency of a known profile is determined, it is possible to estimate the chance that two people selected from a given population at random would have exactly the same profile. This chance is conventionally known as the 'match probability' or the 'random match probability'. The 2004–2005 Annual Report of the NDNAD commented that if all SGM Plus® markers are assumed to be independent then the probability of finding a match between two unrelated persons would be 1 in a trillion. However, since population data still remain somewhat limited, 'it is usual practice to quote a robust and cautious match probability of 1 in a billion'.

It is widely acknowledged that there are many instances in which it may be impossible to construct full genetic profiles from crime scene evidence since the biological samples obtained may be degraded by a number of environmental and temporal factors. Such degradations can lead to a failure to amplify alleles at one or several of the relevant loci, and this will mean that only a partial profile may be obtained. Clearly the chance that a partial profile will match other such partial profiles is much higher than the chance of randomly matching full profiles. Depending on the number of loci that can reliably be measured, partial profiles may match dozens, hundreds or even thousands of those held on a database. This means that, where partial matches may need to be followed up as part of an investigative trajectory, other information may have to be relied on to restrict an otherwise impractically large list of individuals of interest. The most obvious of these relate to the age and geographical location of the individuals concerned, but other circumstantial details more relevant to the specific crime of interest may also be used to determine which partial matches may be used to develop further lines of inquiry.

Likelihood ratios, evidential reasoning and statistical fallacies

Early discussions among forensic scientists in the FSS and between the Home Office and the FSS quickly meant that a 'nationally agreed form of words was devised for describing chance associations from 1:200 to 1 in many millions' (Home Office 1988: 10). Despite changes in the numbers to be included in that calculation as the number of loci sampled increased, and in situations where less than full profiles are obtained, the form of words agreed in the 1980s remains the largely unaltered basis of the expression of such findings in contemporary investigative and judicial contexts in the UK.

However, the same data that provide the basis for a calculation of match probability – the frequency of a given profile genotype in a relevant population as a whole – also provide the basis for the calculation of a more complex, contested and sometimes misunderstood statistical term of art, that of the 'likelihood ratio'. The 'likelihood ratio' provides a numerical representation of the probability of occurrence of two different events – how much more likely is it that one event rather than another would have occurred. In the case of DNA profile evidence obtained from biological material left at a specific crime scene, two events may be hypothesised, and the hypotheses compared by reference to such a likelihood ratio. One hypothesis would be that the individual under suspicion left their biological material, and that is why a profile obtained directly from them matches with the crime scene profile. An alternative hypothesis is that the material left at the crime scene was left by someone else. If the first hypothesis is true then the probability of a match between the two profiles is 1.0; if the second hypothesis is true, then the probability of a match between the two profiles is what has been described already as the random match probability. The likelihood ratio between these two events can easily be calculated. If for example in this case, the random match probability is 1 in one billion, then the hypothesis that the evidence originated from the suspect is one billion times more likely than the alternative hypothesis – that it originated from another person.

Questions raised by the House of Lords Select Committee in 1993 about the presentation of DNA evidence in court revealed significant points of tension within English jurisprudence. Despite the efforts of the FSS to standardise the statistical presentation of evidence a problem arose in two criminal cases, heard in the Court of Appeal in 1994. Both cases – R *v* Deen (1994) and R *v* Gordon (1995) – were appeals that challenged the presentation of DNA evidence in original trials; the appeals were successful and the cases were ordered for re-trial. Both appellants were arrested during a single investigation of a series of rapes, although they were charged with having attacked different victims.

In R *v* Deen the central point of appeal was the statistical presentation of evidence to the jury. At Deen's original trial the DNA 'match probability' was presented as 1 in three million. The evidence was given to the court in the following manner:

> Counsel: So the likelihood of this being any other man but Andrew Deen is one in three million?
> Expert: In three million, yes. (quoted in Redmayne, 2001: 58)

The central problem raised by the expert's answer is that it creates an ambiguity between the probability that the defendant's DNA matched the crime scene profile and the probability that the defendant was the person who left his DNA at the crime scene. The first statistical calculation is based on the random match probability – that is, the probability of finding anyone else within a defined population with the same profile as the defendant. In contrast, the second calculation seems to give (in this case a spurious) quantitative form to the 'likelihood' that Deen committed the crime. This problem with the statistical presentation of evidence has since become known as 'the prosecutor's fallacy' and is based on a misconception – not always deliberately created by the prosecution – that a random match probability is the same as a likelihood ratio.[3]

R *v* Deen demonstrated that the confusion between likelihood ratios and match probabilities can result in misleading statistical assertions in court. Yet, as Redmayne (2001) and others (e.g. Nobles and Schiff 2007) have argued, this is often because likelihood ratios are themselves extremely difficult for a jury to understand. This was apparent in two successive appeals made by Dennis John Adams in the Court of Appeal (R *v* Adams 1996 and 1998). The case against Adams, for rape, was based wholly on DNA evidence (something which has remained unusual because of a 'precautionary principle' which has stressed the need to use DNA only where corroborating evidence is available). He was convicted on the basis of a match probability of 1 in two hundred million. At Adams's original trial his defence introduced a Bayesian likelihood ratio to show how unlikely it was, despite the DNA evidence, that Adams had committed the offence.

In Adams's case the DNA match was the only evidence the prosecution presented. Nevertheless, two other pieces of evidence favoured Adams's defence: first, the victim failed to identify Adams in an identity parade and subsequently stated at a committal hearing that he did not look like the attacker; second, Adams had an alibi (supplied by his girlfriend). The defence, in directing the jury to a Bayesian calculation of Adams's guilt, sought to require a consideration of the significance of these other items of evidence alongside that of the DNA profile match. They also proposed a Bayesian approach to this consideration according to which probabilities can be assigned to the occurrence of each evidential item on the basis of the two hypotheses of innocence and guilt. The two resulting summary probabilities are expressed as a likelihood ratio to support a verdict of guilt or innocence. This method did not persuade the original trial jury and Adams was convicted. Adams appealed on the grounds that the trial judge had failed adequately to direct the jury in how to perform this line of reasoning and, therefore, that his conviction was unsafe. His appeal was allowed and he was retried and convicted again. Adams appealed on the same grounds for a second time.

The Court, on hearing Adams's second appeal, dismissed it. The use of this form of statistical reasoning was strongly deprecated, echoing the judgment of the earlier appeal: 'To introduce Bayes Theorem, or any similar method, into a criminal trial plunged the jury into inappropriate and unnecessary realms of theory and complexity deflecting them from their proper task' (R v Adams 1988: 384). Steventon has subsequently argued that:

In Adams, the defence were too ambitious in their assessment of what the jury could reasonably be expected to understand. The most important message that they were trying to portray concerned the link between the prior odds, the likelihood ratio and the posterior odds; on reflection this could be achieved verbally rather than numerically and it may be more acceptable to the courts. (1998: 184)

Yet Redmayne (2001) argues that these kinds of translations of statistical formulations into verbal statements are also inadequate and so it remains an unhelpful way of presenting evidence to jurors. His assessment is based on a wider consideration of how jurors process and consider the multiplicity of evidence in a criminal case; jurors do not, he argues, formulate evidence in relation to the probabilistic model offered by Bayesian theory. Redmayne argues that it is not that jurors cannot learn Bayesian calculations but that they are not trained in how to integrate those calculations within their usual methods of determining innocence or guilt. A similar view, more prosaically put, was offered by one of the appeal judges during the second Adams appeal when he distinguished between a statistical approach and a normal approach of reasoning (asserting the view that juries follow 'naturalistic' patterns of reasoning rather than mathematical formulae).

The problem with likelihood ratio calculations, therefore, is that they demand a degree of expert reasoning which is problematic for jurors. For this reason it is match probabilities, or 'frequency calculations', that remain the preferred method for the statistical presentation of evidence within court. In a ruling by the Court of Appeal, in the case of R v Doheny and Adams (1996), the court made specific recommendations for how such frequencies should be presented in order to avoid confusion and lend appropriate weight to the forensic evidence. They argued that:

The scientist should not be asked his opinion on the likelihood that it was the Defendant who left the crime stain, nor when giving evidence should he use terminology which may lead the Jury to believe that he is expressing such an opinion. (R v Doheny and Adams 1996)

The Court of Appeal also outlined a standard textual template for the presentation of DNA evidence to a jury:

Members of the Jury, if you accept the scientific evidence called by the Crown, this indicates that there are probably only four or five males in the United Kingdom from whom that semen stain could have come. The Defendant is one of them. If that is the position, the decision you have to reach, on all the evidence, is whether you are sure that it was the Defendant who left that stain or whether it is possible that it was one of that other small group of men who share the same DNA characteristics. (R v Doheny and Adams 1996)

This template enshrines the idea that DNA evidence should not be regarded as providing a definitive match between a suspect and a crime scene, let alone a method of calculating guilt. Rather, DNA evidence may be treated as a method for calculating the probability that a suspect was present at a crime scene from which, in relation to other forms of evidence, it is possible to formulate a verdict of innocence or guilt. While this template has become the basis for the now routine presentation of DNA evidence in court, Redmayne (2001) contends that there are inherent problems in using frequencies in this way. First, the description of match probability tends to convert expectation into precise figures because it leads the jury to believe that probabilistic calculations of match occurrences are factual. Second, if the match is calculated as a small probability, for example 1 in two hundred million, it is difficult to argue that there is another suspect available in the population other than the accused. Thirdly, the choice of the suspect population used to calculate the match is open to question (the judge in Doheny and Adams suggested the 'Caucasian sexually active males in the Manchester area' as the relevant population basis for the calculation of statistical probability, which is a population whose numbers would be difficult to calculate with any degree of certainty). Finally, unlike likelihood ratios, match probabilities tend to allow DNA evidence to outweigh other forms of evidence.

Nevertheless, for the moment it seems that UK courts have settled on conventions for the presentation of DNA evidence that are thought to be responsive both to relevant scientific principles and to lay understandings of probability statistics. While a Bayesian framework may be preferred by some laboratory forensic scientists, including many of those who provide operational intelligence and advice to police investigators, it seems unlikely that this form of reasoning will reappear in the courtroom and be welcomed by judges or advocates. Whether these current conventions will withstand damaging official critiques of the recent use of statistics by other expert witnesses in the courts of England and Wales remains to be seen. In many ways the high quality of the debate about statistics in forensic genetics may have thrown into relief the quality of such a debate in other fields of forensic science.

Conclusion

Our aim in this chapter has been to show how DNA profiling was established as an authoritative and robust tool for both investigative and prosecutorial purposes. The combination of the initial successful police applications and its acceptance in court as reliable evidence meant that, by the early 1990s, DNA profiling was established as a key forensic technology. In relation to the evidential problems which we have described above it is important to remember that these cases are rare examples of challenges to DNA evidence. They are important because as individual and isolated incidences they highlight both a conspicuous lack of legal objections to DNA evidence in England and Wales and the speed at which evidential problems were resolved. This was of central importance for the future establishment and operation of the NDNAD and, as we argue in the next chapter, provided the foundations of credibility and reliability on which to incorporate DNA profiling into routine police work.

Notes

1 Such visual records posed problems since the comparison of similarities and variations between bands necessary to determine whether the samples had a common origin was based on visual and qualitative interpretation. In early uses of the technology there were no agreed or definitive criteria for identifying such matches and laboratories differed in their interpretation of the images. This led to the most significant early dispute regarding DNA fingerprinting in the United Stated where, in New York *v.* Castro (1989), the interpretation of DNA fingerprint matches was shown to be scientifically variable and therefore evidentially contentious.

2 Cellmark Diagnostics trademarked the term 'DNA Fingerprint' and began to offer RFLP services to police in the UK and the USA from 1987 onwards (albeit in competition with Lifecodes, another US laboratory provider).

The effect of the commercial rivalry between these two providers of DNA technology on the history of DNA evidence in US trials is too large a topic to be considered here. Interested readers can consult a substantial US literature on this topic. See especially Thompson (1997), Lynch and Jasanoff (1998) and Lazer (2004).

3 There is a large and complex literature on this topic. See for example: Thompson and Schumann (1987), Redmayne (2001), Roberts and Zuckerman (2004). While the Crown Prosecution Service of England and Wales recognises the existence of this error in reasoning by use of the formal label, it is interesting to note that some English judges have taken a different view. For example, in the October 2000 hearing of the first appeal against the conviction of Sally Clarke for the murder of her two sons, the Appeal judges found the use of the term 'prosecutors fallacy' unnecessary on the grounds that it was 'stating the obvious' to say that the 'probability of two deaths given innocence' was not equivalent to 'the probability of innocence given two deaths' (see Hill 2007: 3).

Chapter 4

Criminalistics and forensic genetics

Introduction

In the previous chapter we described the trajectory of DNA profiling from its scientific origins, through its first operational uses in policing, to the establishment of the technology as a robust investigative and prosecutorial resource. The 'story' of DNA profiling is essentially a story of its successful incorporation into the existing repertoire of identification technologies used within the criminal justice systems of the UK. It is the latest of many efforts to capture and catalogue human individuality for the purposes of both criminal investigation and social administration. The increasingly widespread use of DNA profiling, as we showed in the previous chapter, is attributable to the persuasive combination of its demonstrated scientific validity and reliability, the presumption of its seeming investigative potential, and the readiness of its judicial acceptability.

What has also been crucial in securing the status of DNA profiling within the UK's criminal justice systems is a number of technical and operational innovations which have made it possible for DNA profiling to be routinely incorporated into the work of crime scene examiners and laboratory scientists who collect, analyse and interpret physical evidence in support of criminal investigations in these jurisdictions. While the establishment of a database of searchable DNA profiles taken from known individuals is one necessary precondition for harnessing the potential contribution of forensic genetics to criminal investigations, its effective use also depends heavily on the successful collection of relevant biological material from a sufficient range and number of crime scenes. The increasingly successful deployment of DNA databases everywhere depends upon an organisational capacity to collect the material from such scenes, as well as the technological facility to extract DNA speedily from such materials and subsequently construct usable profiles from the extractions.

In this chapter we outline the current capacity of UK forensic scientists to derive DNA profiles from a variety of biological materials recovered from scenes of crime. We go on to consider recent forensic genetics research which promises to provide intelligence to investigators even when profiles derived from biological material fail to match subject profiles held on a database.

Crime scene examination, physical evidence and forensic intelligence

The systematic forensic investigation of crime scenes involves the application of a range of methods and procedures intended to order physical space in an attempt to discover, secure and analyse selected objects within it. Based on information derived from the application of these resources, inferences are made regarding the source and nature of human actions that may be relevant to a criminal investigation. The term 'crime scene' is used to refer to a number of procedures carried out on different physical and temporal objects and locations including:

a piece of land or part of a street; a building, or a room within a building; the houses, vehicles, vessel and other property of a suspect, witness, or victim; stolen or recovered property; the body, personal possessions and clothing of a suspect, witness or victim; ambulances or other vehicles used to convey victims or offenders to hospital premises, police stations or mortuaries. (Association of Chief Police Officers 2005: 12)

The repertoire of methods and procedures for the investigation of such crime scenes, and the material technologies on which they depend, are central to the discipline of 'criminalistics'. The American Academy of Forensic Sciences defines criminalistics as 'that profession and scientific discipline directed to the recognition, identification, individualization and evaluation of physical evidence by application of the physical sciences to law-science matters' (quoted in Nickell and Fischer 1999: 2). The discipline has its formal origins in late nineteenth and early twentieth century European textbooks on 'scientific' crime investigation and was given particular attention by Gross in his treatise *Criminal Investigation* first published in 1892.

Criminalistics has become clearly differentiated from its neighbouring discipline, criminology. For example, Sekula (1986) has contrasted the image of criminologists as 'scientists of crime', interested in the knowledge and mastery of *criminality* in general, with that of criminalists as 'technicians of crime', interested in gaining the knowledge and mastery of individual *criminals* and their actions. For Ginzburg (1980, 1983, 1990), the emergence of such an occupational practice represented a conjunction of longstanding semiotic and conjectural forms of practical reasoning 'oriented to the analysis of specific cases which could be reconstructed only through traces, symptoms and clues' (1990: 104) (methods familiar to historians, physicians and other specialist occupational groups) and the rigorous formal reasoning typical of the natural sciences. There have been many other attempts to describe the 'elastic rigour' (Ginzburg 1980:28) that characterises the epistemological and methodological preferences that inform both early and contemporary criminalistic practices. Such practices are widely recognised to combine a range of scientific and technical procedures with extensive tacit and weakly articulated knowledge of individual cases and their local contexts. Typically, there is a recognition that criminalistics lacks the codification, coordination and systematisation required to set it on a firm theoretical foundation, but that it comprises a 'large assortment of effective technical procedures' (Kirk 1963: 235).

While the term 'criminalistics' does not have general currency in the UK, the work of individuals known variously as 'scenes of crime officers', 'crime scene examiners', or 'crime scene investigators' (as well as the cadre of more specialised forensic scientists who may examine particular scenes of crime) exhibits all the features of this hybrid conjectural/scientific occupation and shares the fundamental objective of providing reliable scientific results to support the investigation of crime (Netzel 2003: 164). Members of this group are characterised by their knowledge of a set of investigative routines, their use of a range of methods for the identification, collection and preservation of physical material, their orientation to the examination of scenes of crime for the purpose of reconstructing previously committed actions, and their common vocabulary for the description and evaluation of their work. As we suggested earlier, a longstanding and central pre-occupation of this work has been to provide and interpret material (including biological) traces left at crime scenes in order to 'individualise' the person who left such traces. For this reason technical progress in the quality and quantity of resources available to accomplish such an outcome (sometimes called 'identification', sometimes 'individuation') has been central to the actual or imagined expansion of their contribution to criminal investigations (Kirk 1963).

Sources and amounts of biological material

Forensic science and criminalistics journals and texts have reported and summarised a wide range of research studies on developments in the collection, analysis and accounting of DNA profiles in support of criminal investigations since the late 1980s. A few years after the publication of the first papers on DNA profiling, and at a time when his own work had shown that the hybridisation probes in common use required large quantities of human DNA (50ng for single locus probes and 0.1 to 1 µg for multi-locus probes), Jeffreys et al. (1988) published an article suggesting future possibilities for obtaining forensic DNA profiles from quantities as low as single cells recovered from crime scenes. The paper reported the results of the analysis of single nucleated cell droplets and demonstrated that minisatellite alleles could be detected by Southern blot hybridisation following the use of TAq polymerase in PCR amplifications of between 10 and 25 cycles (although at cycle numbers above 20 significant problems arose in the quality of PCR products). The paper suggested that:

As a guide, 10–15 cycles are appropriate for 100ng genomic DNA in a 10 µl PCR reaction, 10–15 cycles for 1 ng DNA and 25 cycles for single cell PCR (6pg). The number of PCR cycles may need to be increased to detect larger alleles which amplify less efficiently. (p.10967)

Jeffreys and his colleagues argued that this technological potential widened immensely the range of objects that scene examiners could treat as potential sources of DNA material – e.g. 'trace amounts of hair, blood, semen, saliva and urine' (p. 10969). They noted that this simultaneously increased the potential for the contamination of such profiles at the scene and in the subsequent laboratory handling of the material: 'The potential for inadvertent contamination of specimens ... is likewise evident' (p. 10969).

Almost ten years after Jeffreys' original paper, Findley et al. (1997)

obtained profiles from single cells using the standard SGM system currently in use by the FSS, having increased the number of PCR cycles to 34. Results were obtained from 91 per cent of the 226 cells analysed and from these full STR profiles were obtained in one-half of the cases and partial profiles obtained in a further 27 per cent. However, even when the technology was applied to the analysis of buccal cells obtained directly from donors, the authors also reported that a significant number of the profiles yielded contained additional alleles either in conjunction with 'true' alleles, or in place of 'true' alleles, and that allele dropout occurred in 39 per cent of the cells analysed using this methodology. For this reason, findings were seen to require modified systems of interpretation and a corresponding degree of caution appropriate to their uses in forensic casework.

Since the biological material used for the experimental procedures reported in these early papers was usually obtained directly from human subjects, the suggestion that the analysis of crime scene material of the kind described above could also be successful remained a theoretical possibility rather than an empirical accomplishment. But one clear feature of the trajectory of DNA profiling since the late 1980s has been the increasing success of forensic laboratories at being able to obtain analysable quantitites and qualities of DNA from an increasing variety of sources. These include 'trace' or 'touch' DNA from 'dead epidermal cells that have sloughed off the skin surface and been carried onto a secondary surface by sweat or abrasion' (Bright and Petricevic 2004: 7). In the early 1990s, Wiegand and his associates were able to derive and profile DNA from debris obtained from fingernail scrapings (Wiegand *et al.* 1993) and later from epithelial cells left on a victim's body following strangulation (Wiegand and Kleiber 1997, 1998), as well as cells left on strangulation tools (Wiegand *et al.* 2000). Abaz *et al.* (2002) obtained DNA from drinking vessels, and similar success was reported in efforts to type DNA obtained from clothing textiles and by tape-liftings from fabric shoe insoles (see Schultz and Reichert 2000 and Bright and Petricevic 2004). Successful DNA typing from dandruff (e.g. Herber and Herold 1998) and saliva retained on cigarette butts has been carried out for some time (e.g. Watanabe *et al.* 2003).

A number of forensic researchers have reported similar success at obtaining STR profiles from trace DNA. However, many of these studies were based on amounts of DNA equivalent to hundreds of cells and often reported success at identifying only a single locus. Several studies (e.g. van Oorschot and Jones 1997; van Oorschot *et al.* 1998; van Hoofstdt 1998; van Rentergeum 2000) reported DNA typing from 'fingerprints', 'touched objects' or 'skin debris', or more accurately, from 'swabs taken from objects touched by hands'. In the earliest of these papers (van Oorschot *et al.* 1998), alleles at a single STR locus were successfully recovered from a range of touched objects including leather briefcase handles, pens, a car key, a personal locker handle and a telephone handset (all regularly handled by specific individuals), as well as from other objects that had been cleaned before being held for a short period of time by a single individual (including plastic knife handles, a mug, a glass, and a pair of vinyl gloves).

While such single locus profiling might be useful for eliminating individuals from further inquiry, the combination of stochastic effects and the potential for inadvertent contamination when using high numbers of PCR cycles were recognised to cause major problems in the reliability of measurements and thus the robustness of such uses of DNA profiling. Furthermore, it is widely recognised that trace DNA can be transferred directly from skin contact between persons and indirectly through consecutive contact with inert surfaces and objects (see, for example, Lowe *et al.* 2002). For example, in the case of DNA recovered from fingermarks that have been revealed by the application of fingerprint powder, it is possible that cellular material has been transferred to the mark of interest by a brush that had been used to develop previous marks (see Sutherland *et al.* 2002; Wickenhieser 2002; Buckleton and Gill 2005).

Despite these challenges, however, DNA analysis using an increased number of amplification cycles has been used successfully in forensic science casework in the UK since 1999 (Buckleton and Gill 2005: 276). A large number of studies have been reported on the actual and potential uses of such 'low copy number' (LCN) analysis. For example, Balogh *et al.* (2003) reported experimental research on the successful production of ten loci profiles (those included in the Profile Plus™ Kit) derived from 28, 32, and 38 cycle PCR amplifications of DNA extracted from 'fingerprints' left on paper. High rates of correctly typed profiles (checked against reference profiles from relevant individuals) were obtained from samples made under a variety of conditions. Correctly typed profiles were obtained from 80 per cent of swabs taken from paper, from more than 86 per cent of samples of cut paper, and from 47 per cent of fingermarks treated with chemical enhancers prior to DNA analysis. The authors also argued that increasing the number of PCR cycles from 28 and 32 cycles to 38 cycles PCR did not significantly increase artefact and stutter incidence, although loci in the multiplex with longer fragment lengths were more vulnerable to allelic drop-out and drop-in than those with shorter lengths. In addition, they remind the potential user of such methods that secondary or tertiary transfer of genetic material is known to be common and is likely to complicate DNA typing of this kind of cellular material.

Information from all of these – and many other – studies has been drawn on by the providers of DNA forensic profiling services to issue advice to crime scene investigators about the likelihood of obtaining DNA profiles from a wide range of material and fluids that might be found and recovered from crime scenes. Constant innovations in such technologies rapidly make redundant any summary of current scientific capability. However, examination of several recent sources of this informed advice to crime scene investigators about the discovery and submission of material indicates a common understanding of what is worth collecting and why. The following paragraphs summarise this advice drawn from documents published by the Forensic Science Service (1994, 2003) and The Association of Chief Police Officers (2004, 2005).

Blood found in varying quantities of liquid or dried blood at crime scenes, is recovered by swabbing or scraping. Since it shares its appearance with a number of other fluids, investigators are encouraged to conduct presumptive tests for its presence before sampling what might seem to be old dried blood stains. Figures produced by the Forensic Science Service in 2003 gave the success rates of obtaining DNA from blood at 84 per cent.

Semen (rich in DNA contained in spermatozoa and with a successful DNA recovery rate of 90 per cent) can also be found in liquid form or more usually as a dried stain. When it is possible that dried semen is present – on clothing or other fabrics – but is invisible to the naked eye, another presumptive test may be used to reveal its presence before it is collected for analysis. It may also be recovered from discarded condoms.

While **saliva** does not contain DNA itself, cheek cells are shed (in variable amounts) into saliva and can be processed to obtain DNA. There are many potential sources of saliva (even when liquid or dried saliva is not immediately visible), including cigarette and cigar butts (with a cigarette recovery rate of 75 per cent), gags, balaclavas, drinking vessels and containers, postage stamps and envelopes, toothbrushes, and partially eaten food. Forensic Science Service figures show that DNA can be recovered from 94 per cent of chewing gum samples submitted, and they cite an overall recovery rate of 40 per cent from 'saliva samples' in 2003.

Hair roots and scalp cells contain DNA and may typically be found 'trapped in the shoes of someone who has kicked a victim; caught between surfaces at a point of entry; pulled out by a victim in a struggle with the offender; on a weapon; on a vehicle in a road traffic accident/collision; inside a balaclava worn by an individual' (ACPO 2005: 16). Recent figures for successful recovery from rooted hair stand at 50 per cent, and hair without visible roots at 15 per cent.

Flesh, skin and body parts contain varying amounts of cellular material. Pieces of flesh and body parts are likely to obtain large quantities of DNA except where they are badly decomposed (and even then they may be sufficient for analysis). Surface layers of skin will normally require LCN profiling. The FSS are successful at obtaining DNA from 69 per cent of fingernail clippings and from 18 per cent of watch straps submitted for analysis. Finger rings have also been found to be useful sources of DNA.

Vaginal fluid containing cells from the lining of the vagina may be collected from items at crimes scenes and (by medically qualified personnel) from penile swabs taken from suspects. In either case it is likely to be mixed with seminal fluid and so a mixed profile is likely to result. This means that laboratory and/or statistical methods will be necessary to separate out the profiles and interpret their significance in the case in question.

Nasal secretions found in discarded handkerchiefs or other material are regarded as a good sources of DNA.

Dandruff which consists of dried skin tissue is less good, though it could be collected and submitted for DNA analysis if the circumstances seem to warrant it.

Neither **urine** nor **faeces** are understood to provide a good source of DNA. However, the former may contain skin cells detached from the urethra, and faeces may be mixed with blood or may contain rectal cells. In these circumstances DNA profiles may be obtainable and mitochondrial DNA profiling is often used for the analysis of faecal material. For this reason, crime scene examiners may on occasions collect these types of biological material and submit them for laboratory analysis.

Scientific innovations

The routine uses of genetic information in support of policing largely depend on matching profiles obtained from scenes of crime to the profiles of individuals already held on databases (or sometimes to the profiles of individuals who have supplied biological samples in the course of an investigation). However, there are many investigations in which genetic material has been recovered from a crime scene but no such matches have been made. In such circumstances, investigators may seek other ways to identify such individuals using their DNA sample. New forms of genetic knowledge, technological improvements in sample processing, and the perceived rewards of investigative ingenuity, mean that there are constant innovations in methods for interrogating the informational content of biological samples obtained from scenes of crime. The capacity to analyse unidentified genetic samples for content that can yield identifying information has continued to grow over the last decade. At present, analysis can be undertaken to gain information about phenotypical attributes, 'bio-geographic ancestry' and 'familial relationships'. Some interrogations involve the direct examination of coding regions of the human genome – genes themselves – while others rely on new ways of using information from the non-coding areas already examined by conventional forensic genotyping.

The successful application of such innovations to specific criminal cases – especially 'hard-to-solve' cases – often becomes the subject of widespread media attention, but the trajectories of such implementation are usually more complex and uncertain than may appear from newspaper and broadcast accounts. The research base for these developments has typically been in specialist forensic laboratories or in private biotech companies. However, in some cases – at least in the UK – independent academic research, carried out by particular individuals or small research groups and supported by research councils or charities, has also provided significant scientific and technological resources. In many of these latter cases, novel techniques or approaches have been commended for their potential to resolve a variety of specific investigative uncertainties. These emerging forms of 'genetic intelligence' are not aimed at providing forensic evidence for use in judicial hearings but, rather, are expected to provide law enforcers with actionable information for the purposes of criminal investigation (albeit information of varying degrees of exactitude). Because of the additional resources currently required to deploy some of these genetic interrogations many of them, even in jurisdictions that allow their use, will not be incorporated into routine police inquiries in the forseeable future. Nevertheless, we describe some of them here since they raise new practical, policy and ethical issues for those involved and interested in the use of genetic information for crime investigation.

'Genetic ancestry', 'population groups' and forensic investigations

One particularly complex area of genetic information of interest to criminal investigators has been that of patterned human genetic diversity. Knowledge of the differential variability of genotypes according to population groups has been relevant to the calculation of random match probabilities since the early days of DNA profiling. While the details of population genetics are largely of interest to the specialised forensic community, the ability to infer the population origin of an otherwise unidentified crime scene stain is of significant interest to investigators: specifically, the possibility of relating this genetic knowledge to lay characterisations of the 'racial origins', 'ethnic origin' 'ethnic affiliation' or even 'ethnic appearance' of individuals. Reliable inferences of this kind can be used to focus subsequent inquiries, to determine an interview strategy, to compare with witness statements, or to design an intelligence-led mass DNA screen.

There are, of course, many conceptual and operational uncertainties surrounding the 'ethnic estimation' of individuals whose biological material has been recovered from scenes of crime. Moreover, there is a danger, well articulated by Duster (2003, 2004, 2005), Cho and Sankar (2004, 2005) and others, that 'race' will be reified in the attempt to define distinctive human population groups and subgroups. These critics also point to the ways in which questions of genetic 'ancestral attribution' for these limited and pragmatic purposes can easily become confused with more ambitious theoretical assertions concerning the biology of 'race' as well as 'some old and dangerously regressive ideas about how to explain criminal conduct' (Duster 2003: 151).

Despite these problems, a number of forensic laboratories and agencies have added to their analysis of autosomal DNA STRs and SNPs, Y-chromosome STR and Y-chromosome SNP multiplexes for the analysis of loci whose polymorphic range is already databased by a variety of international consortia. The Y chromosome is an especially suitable site for such investigations because of the low rate of recombination on this chromosome. This means that particular male-specific haplotypes are preserved across generations and vary systematically across different population groups (see Jobling and Tyler-Smith 1995; Jobling *et al.* 1997 and Jobling 2001 for accounts of this). Thus there are several ways in which these systematic variations have been examined in forensic contexts.

Autosomal STRs and 'ethnic inference'

Lowe *et al.* (2001) have described the methodology used by the UK's Forensic Science Service for inferring the 'ethnic origin' of DNA samples profiled using the second generation multiplex test SGM which comprises the analysis of six loci and amelogenin. Based on previous work using RFLP analysis carried out by Evett *et al.* (1992), as well as on SGM by Evett *et al.* (1997), the method estimates the proportion of any profiled genotype found among five ethnically differentiated British sub-populations ('Caucasian', 'Afro-Caribbean', 'Indian Sub-continental', 'Southeast Asian' and 'Middle Easterners'). These are the ethnic designations used by the police and recorded together with genetic profiles obtained from individuals whose DNA was sampled on arrest. Their results showed that analysis of the six autosomal STR loci provided designations of population of origin that were correct in only 56 per cent of those described as 'Caucasians', 67 per cent of those described as 'Afro-Caribbeans' and 43 per cent of 'South Asians'.

The authors are careful to note that dependence on such designations affects the validity of potential inferences and that the method is a probabilistic rather than a categorical one. However, it is not clear that they fully recognise the problems that surround the theoretical underpinning of such an approach. This can be seen in their claim that 'the composition of the databases cannot be regarded as ethnically pure' (Lowe *et al.* 2001: 21). Such a comment is problematic because of its confusing use of 'ethnicity' in relation to 'purity'. Even if another term was substituted for 'ethnicity' it would remain analogous to modern societies in which there are few 'geographically localized, reproductively isolated groups(s)' (Duster 2005: 1051) representing any simple ethnic 'purity'.

Y-chromosome STRs

Recent years have seen a substantial expansion in the use of Y chromosome STR markers for the analysis of crime scene samples.

While one use of such Y STR markers has been for the interpretation of mixed male/female biological samples (e.g. those collected during the investigation of rapes and other sexual assaults) they can also be interrogated to infer the 'specific population group' to which genetic material is affiliated. Such inferences are based on the use of existing evidence of both distinctive and shared paternal lineage among specific population groups. Among the research and reference databases that provide such evidence are the Y-STR haplotype reference database (www.yhrd.org), the US population database (www.ystr. org/usa), and a European population database (www.ysrt.charite. de). Although studies that have used Y-chromosome haplotypes to infer the 'racial origin' of samples have produced seemingly more 'accurate' results than the studies reported in the previous sub-section, there are still many problems in both the assumptions that underlie them and the pragmatics of their use in forensic contexts. For example, Syndercombe-Court *et al.* (2003) report that halotype evidence 'correctly identified' 80 per cent, 72 per cent and 89 per cent of individuals who had defined themselves and both parents as 'White', 'Black' or 'South Asian').

Autosomal Single Nucleotide Polymorphisms (SNPs)

There are believed to be ten million SNPs in the human genome. According to Sobrino *et al.* (2005: 1): 'more than 5 million SNPs have been collected and around 4 million SNPs have been validated, this it to say they have been confirmed to be polymorphic in one or various major population groups'. There have been several surveys of SNP polymorphisms, many of which are collected together in a global haplotype map known as the 'HapMap' (www.hapmap.org). SNPs have a much more limited polymorphic range than STRs, so that about four times as many SNPs are needed to produce profiles, capable of discriminating individuality, as those used by STR typing (Gill 2001; Sobrino *et al.* 2005). There are a number of different SNP typing technologies. However, many of them have limited multiplexing capability and, because of this, are unlikely to be the technologies of choice for the routine analysis of crime scene samples. While rapid developments in this field may alter this possibility (Sobrino *et al.* 2005), the current expert view is that SNPs are unlikely to replace STRs for large scale forensic databasing in the foreseeable future (Gill *et al.* 2004).

Nevertheless, the establishment and expansion of SNP forensic databases alongside current STR collections are not out of the question. Despite problems with SNPs their analytical scope means that they can serve valuable forensic identification functions, especially in situations where samples are too degraded to make STR typing possible. Frudakis *et al.* (2003) have suggested that recent research on more than 200 autosomal SNPs shows that 56 of them differed between 'three major race groups' and can therefore be used to infer 'racial origins'. Indeed, this research has been used to add credibility to the commercial genotyping service provided by Genomics Inc. of Sarasota, Florida, and there have been a small number of high-profile criminal inquiries in the USA to which this company has contributed.

Y-chromosome SNPs

The Y Chromosome Consortium (2002) has provided a 'phylogenetic tree' which describes the history of 18 major lineages of diverse SNP haplotypes across human populations. Jobling (2001), Vallone and Butler (2004), Wetton *et al.* (2005) and others have recently discussed the development and use of Y-SNP multiplexes to support inferences of population origin. In the study by Wetton *et al.* (2005) samples obtained from the UK's NDNAD and from volunteer donors were SNP typed on 43 loci to assign each individual to one of the 18 lineages. These assignations were subsequently compared to the visual classifications made of 627 donors, implementing the full repertoire of six 'ethnic appearance' categories used by the police (pale-skinned Caucasian, dark-skinned Caucasian, African/Afro-Caribbean, Indian Sub-continent, East Asian and North African/Middle Eastern). When a comparison was made between the assignment of each individual to one of these groups on the basis of visual appearance and the assignment on the basis of Y-SNP inference, there was high but variable concordance. The spread ranged from a low of 74 per cent of concordant assignments to the Indian Sub-continent ethnic appearance category, to a high of 88 per cent of concordant assignments to the pale-skinned Caucasian ethnic appearance category. Once again, the researchers note the contribution to admixtures to failures to concordant assignment, recommend the use of such Y Chromosome SNP haplotyping in combination with other tests of biogenetic ancestry (e.g. mitochondrial sequence data, autosomal STRs), and conclude that useful rather than definitive intelligence can be derived for investigators.

At present it is difficult to adequately evaluate the significance of these various efforts to provide information about genetic ancestry.

A clear preference for SNPs markers over STRs seems to have emerged over the last few years and large numbers of SNPs are now combined to form 'ancestry informative markers', some of which have been used in forensic casework (Shriver *et al*. 2005). However, until recently, there have been problems in standardising such markers and in the standardisation of haplotype nomenclature (Tyler-Smith 1999). It is also reported that the increase in populations of mixed origin is a feature of complex urban societies so that 'indirect deductions about individuals are often unreliable' (Jobling 2001: 161). Even when the pattern of differential SNP distributions is used to 'improve' the accuracy of such inferences, as in the case with 'proportional ancestry' studies, there remain conspicuous uncertainties.

Inferring specific phenotypical features – the 'genetic photofit'

In addition to efforts at identifying the genetic ancestry of unmatched crime scene stains, forensic scientists and police investigators remain interested in whether interrogations of such stains may yield information about the wide repertoire of visible characteristics of their donors. For the purposes of police investigations, the ability to determine directly individuals' physical characteristics may be more appealing than inferring those characteristics from assumptions of biogeographic ancestry. The most frequently used method of direct interrogation – of the amelogenin locus – determines the biological sex of the DNA source and is already incorporated into the majority of multiplex systems. Aside from this test, however, the research literature reveals limited success in attributing phenotype from genotype in ways that are practically useful to investigators.

The UK's *Police Science and Technology Strategy 2003 to 2008* makes a commitment to support the development of research which will 'predict physical characteristics' from DNA, but an initial review of forensic work in this field suggests that positive results remain scare. While analysis of the human melanocortin 1 receptor gene can be used to indicate 'red hair' in the relevant subject (Grimes *et al*. 2001), hair loss and hair colouring can make this test problematic when applied in investigatory contexts. Both STR and SNP profiling are of interest to forensic scientists keen to develop predictive tests for a range of other observable physical characteristics, including eye colour, skin type, and height. It seems likely that SNP analysis may prove more successful than STR markers as the basis for such tests. This is not simply because most genomic mutations are single base changes but also because there is considerable research being carried out beyond the forensic community to identify SNP polymorphisms and their effects on a variety of human attributes. For example DNAPrint Genomics offers 'RETINOME' to forensic investigators in which it is possible to infer eye colour – in part from a 'human pigmentation' gene SNP, along with other ancestral marker SNPs. There may be other such tests available but we know little of their reliability or their practical applicability to criminal investigations.

Familial searching

The term 'familial searching', as used by forensic scientists and police officers in the UK, refers to a form of database searching based on knowledge about the probability of matches between the STR markers of two members of the same family (as opposed to the probability of matches between these markers when the individuals compared are unrelated). This practice makes use of understandings of inheritance that prefigured the discovery of the structure of DNA and which had been largely applied to understanding variation in human, animal and plant phenotypical characteristics (see Bieber 2004, for a summary account of these assumptions as applied to the forensic context). The work of Alec Jeffreys and his colleagues in the 1980s represented an effort to operationalise and test these understandings at the genetic rather than the phenotypic level (see Jeffreys *et al*. 1985). Conceptually, Jeffreys sought both to reliably differentiate individuals from one another and also to establish patterns of variations between those who were genetically related. Jeffreys' research programme had been focused on the development of robust methods for establishing and representing genetic heredity, and the first human application of his technique – then termed 'DNA fingerprinting' – using multi-locus probes, was to assess claims of family connectedness in an immigration case in the UK.

The FSS has considered the utility of database searches based on this knowledge since 1996 and their Forensic Intelligence Bureau now offers police forces in England and Wales a search of the NDNAD to identify possible relatives of criminal suspects. The procedure has been applied when a full DNA profile obtained from a crime scene has not matched an existing full profile on the database. Familial searching utilises the increased likelihood of similarity between the DNA profiles of those who have a direct genetic relationship in order to identify a parent, child or sibling of an individual whose profile is not currently on the database. Familial searching therefore refers not to the *social* arrangement of families, but the genetic relationships between individuals – a distinction which is important for investigative as well as ethical reasons.

Despite several well-publicised instances, applications of familial searching in the UK remain numerically small. In 2004, the FSS reported that approximately 20 familial searches had been undertaken and that a quarter of these had yielded 'useful intelligence information'. In 2005 the government reported that since 2003 the technique had been used 'around' 80 times. The reasons for this limited application include recognition of the novelty of the process and also the volume of partial matches it may provide. Because familial searching relies on identifying a pool of the possible genetic relatives of a suspect, who are then subject to more direct investigation (typically by being interviewed by the police), ACPO has also acknowledged that a number of ethical issues need to be addressed when this strategy is being considered. The *National DNA Database Annual Report 2002–03* stated that the 'Database Board has recently sought advice from the Information Commissioner on the ethics and data protection issues of using this new approach more widely and will be issuing guidelines in the near future' (Forensic Science Service 2003: 25).

While such guidelines have not been issued, their perceived necessity reflects the recognition of several fundamental problems that surround the use of this search procedure to direct investigations. Issues arise in both the searching of profiles on the NDNAD and in the subsequent investigative trajectories that follow the provision of a list of individuals derived from such a search. A genetic link between individuals might be previously unknown by one or both parties and police investigations may make such information known to them for the first time. Equally an investigation may reveal (to investigators – if not to informants) the absence of genetic links which participants assumed to have existed. There is also the question of whether this kind of use of an individual's databased DNA violates promises of privacy and confidentiality made when their genetic material was originally donated voluntarily. Furthermore, assertions about criminality, geography and familial relatedness that are central to the use of this forensic methodology are especially problematic (even if they do accord with the rhetorical endoxa of many detectives). For instance, the Custodian of the NDNAD said in a public meeting of the UK Human Genetics Commission held in February 2004 that '[Familial searching] is based on some very important assumptions that criminality can run in families, that a relative could be on the database, the families tend to live in the same area, and that offenders tend to offend close to their homes or in areas that they frequently visit'. The same assertions are made in the most recent *National DNA Database Annual Report* (Forensic Science Service 2004). Yet they reveal pervasive problems associated with the confusion between 'genetic' and 'social' relatedness ('families' are not only constituted through genetic lines but through clusters of non-genetically related individuals), as well as the implicit assumption that criminality is fostered because of such relatedness (either because of genetic or social reasons).[1]

It is likely that these issues will be widely discussed in the near future whenever it is more widely exploited by the police and more members of the public become involved in sample requests. It may be that legislative and statutory regulations prohibit such searching of databases profiles in many jurisdictions, and also that familial searching is impractical in databases which do not contain large collections of profiles – small archives will obviously provide less scope for making partial matches because of their limited coverage of the population. Nevertheless, familial searching is a forensic practice that is certain to be developed in the future.

Conclusion

Despite its alignment with the generalising physical sciences and the technologies derived from them, criminalistics remains necessarily and resolutely informed by an interest in the application of particular investigatory and analytical techniques to individual (and sometimes to a series of) criminal cases under investigation (Sekula 1986). For this reason, its research traditions and efforts have traditionally been directed towards the improvement of techniques and methods for the delivery of more accurate, more reliable, speedier and cheaper forensic artefacts and providing guidance on the appropriate forensic strategies for use in particular kinds of investigations. Such research has furnished forensic investigators, analysts and other participants with important information about both the benefits and the risks of the use of particular techniques and methodologies, as well as the likelihood that successful profiling can be carried out from differing qualities and quantities of biological material. In addition, research on the genetic information that can be derived from crime scene samples when profiles fail to match suspect profiles currently held on a database provides new resources for investigators.

The recent development of criminalistics in general mirrors (and in many ways depends upon) the recent history of DNA profiling in particular. The dissemination of knowledge of the continuously increasing potential of new and enhanced methods of DNA extraction from biological materials among criminal investigators and crime scene examiners has been a central feature of its successful implementation within policing in the UK. In turn, the integration of DNA profiling into the criminal justice system (based on the ubiquity of its availability, the robustness of methods for its recovery and analysis, and the increasing clarity of probabilistic reasoning about its significance) has meant that new experimental and inferential methods have been developed to deal with many of the practical problems associated with the collection, analysis and interpretation of biological materials in forensic contexts.

All of these scientific and technological advances in the collection and analysis of genetic material from crime scenes are germane to an understanding of the increased use of genetic information in support of policing in the UK and elsewhere. However, we have already indicated in earlier chapters that the ambitions that inform and shape them are political rather than technical, and cultural rather than material. They are driven by a wider forensic imaginary that promotes, as another necessary element, the collection, storage and speculative searching of genetic material taken from known subjects. Accordingly the next chapter returns to a consideration of how and why one such collection – the NDNAD of England and Wales – has taken its current form.

Note

1 Recent – and opposing – commentaries on these matters can be found in Greeley *et al.* (2006) and Haimes (2006).

Chapter 5

Populating the NDNAD – inclusion and contestation

Introduction

This chapter turns attention to the establishment and development of the increasing large and heterogeneous collection of genetic profiles which currently comprises the NDNAD. This register of DNA profiles has been facilitated by a series of inter-related scientific and governmental innovations which have encouraged the police to routinely collect and retain genetic samples from individuals and from scenes of crime. Such databasing is not the inevitable outcome of either developments in the technology of DNA profiling or its successful application to criminal case work. On the contrary, it is a distinct and deliberate activity designed to harness and align the technological capacities of DNA profiling to the governmental agenda of crime detection and crime management which we discussed earlier.

Enabling police forces in England and Wales to construct such a large collection of genetic profiles has required specific legislative arrangements. The historical foundations of this legislative schema can be traced to expert considerations in the early 1990s which inspired amendments to the Police and Criminal Evidence Act (PACE) 1984 to widen the scope of DNA collection within routine policing. This legislative history shows an astonishing set of changes in how the police can obtain and use genetic information without the consent of the individuals from which it was taken. However, these changes have taken place within a contested terrain of deliberations in which a number of competing discourses – from the police, judiciary, expert committees, and human rights groups – have contributed to reshaping the 'balance' between the powers of the police and the rights of individual subjects. We describe this trajectory here in order to show how the development of the database has required a significant number of changes in the discursive construction and regulation of the legal relationship between the human body and the state.

Technological innovation and legal context

In Chapter 3, we described how the initial development of DNA profiling and its use in criminal investigations by the police demonstrated its effectiveness on a case-by-case basis, especially in cases of sexual and violent crime. In this chapter we want to focus on the resulting transition, quickly proposed by a number of key actors within the UK, to the creation of a database of profiles (collected from crime scenes and from known individuals) which could be harnessed for the purpose of searching and comparison whenever any newly obtained profiles were added to it. The initial forensic use of DNA in the 'Pitchfork' case had already demonstrated that the success of the technology depended upon the scope and coverage of the collection of reference profiles to which crime scene samples could be compared. However, in this first use, comparison was only made possible by a long and costly process of intelligence-led screening – something which itself proved, through Colin Pitchfork's initial evasion, to be a problematic method for aiding criminal detection. It is therefore not surprising that, very quickly, the idea of a creating an 'index' of DNA profiles, capable of being searched against crime scene stains, was considered. The Home Office first recorded their interest in such a development in 1988 and began research into developing a database. While the imagined form of this database was limited by the available technology, the potential of this new type of contact trace material was being carefully explored.[1]

The House of Commons Home Affairs Committee, who undertook a systematic assessment of the Forensic Science Service at the end of the 1980s, argued that the development of such a 'DNA index' was highly desirable for both the prevention and detection of crime and the robust authority it could lend to forensic science. The context for this enthusiasm was a criminal justice system in which some applications of forensic evidence in court had damaged public confidence in its reliability. There were also complaints by the police about the quality and the timeliness of forensic science support to investigators.

Against this background the Home Affairs Committee argued that the 'potential of the test in criminal investigation is immense' and that 'DNA profiling represents the opportunity for [a] great advance in forensic scientific detection' (HC Paper 26-I, 1989: xxxii). Yet, while the committee recognised the potential of DNA databasing for police investigations they also noted a 'number of legal problems to be overcome before an index of DNA profiles can be contemplated' (HC Paper 26-I, 1989: xxxii). These 'legal problems' related primarily to the legislative framework through which the police were empowered to obtain a DNA sample from an individual suspect without their consent and subsequently to store it for future use. The government response similarly noted that while work 'is underway to establish a framework for developing a data base of DNA profiles' the 'possible creation of a DNA database also raises important legal and ethical questions' (CM 699, 1989: 8).

The recognition that DNA databasing raises significant social, ethical and legal issues has continually structured the government's approach to facilitating the lawful collection and use of DNA samples and profiles by the police. Significantly, there has never been one legislative instrument or Act of Parliament to establish either the database or the powers of the police on which it relies. Rather, the NDNAD has been facilitated piecemeal by successive amendments to existing legislation, in particular to PACE (1984). To date, there are three elements which characterise a progressively 'layered' set of PACE amendments: first, changes in measures which allow the police to take CJ samples from individuals; second, changes in the provisions which allow the police to retain CJ samples and profiles; and third, changes in the powers granted to the police to speculatively search all retained profiles.

When DNA profiling was first used by the police in England and Wales, PACE (1984) provided the framework under which samples could be taken from individuals. That legislation differentiated between 'intimate' and 'non-intimate' samples. A non-intimate sample was defined as a sample of hair other than pubic hair, a sample taken from a nail or from under a nail, a swab taken from any part of a person's body other than a bodily orifice, a footprint or a similar impression of any part of the body other than a part of the hand (fingerprints were treated separately). An intimate sample, which could not be taken without consent, was defined as a sample of blood, semen or any other tissue, fluid, urine, saliva or pubic hair, or a swab taken from a bodily orifice. Only non-intimate samples could be taken without consent from an individual charged with an offence. Such non-intimate samples could be taken only when a senior police officer had reasonable grounds for believing that the sample would yield significant information relevant to the person's possible involvement in the crime under investigation.

These legislative arrangements, which establish the legal status of the human body and limit police powers to compel suspects to provide certain samples, were quickly seen by government to be problematic in the light of advances in DNA technologies. Enthusiasm for DNA profiling to potentially transform investigative practice by providing an efficient and objective method of detecting suspects and confirming their identities was contrasted with existing legislation which was deemed inhibitive to its successful use. Several agencies speculated on how the police could be enabled to lawfully collect different bodily samples from suspects. For instance, as early as 1987 the *Review of the Scientific Support for the Police*, a report published by the accountants Touche Ross after a study commissioned by the Home Office, argued that 'consideration could be given to seeking a change to make saliva samples non-intimate' but, since this would require a legislative amendment, 'it is probably best, at this stage, to ensure that the power to take hair as a non-intimate sample is maintained' (1987: para 10.4). By 1989 the Home Affairs Select Committee had recommended that the courts should possess the power to order compulsory blood sampling of suspects (pursuant to the Magistrates Courts Act 1980) in cases of serious offences. Although subsequent legislative developments have not relied on the need to allow police to obtain judicial authority to collect blood samples (because blood samples have become unnecessary for producing DNA profiles), the Select Committee's recommendation highlights the early attention given to the issue of non-consensual DNA sampling by the police.

The first reconsideration of the rules governing the taking and storage of bodily samples without consent was by The Royal Commission on Criminal Justice in the early 1990s.[2] When The Royal Commission published its findings and recommendations in 1993, after a comprehensive assessment of the collection and use of evidence across the whole criminal justice system, it was underpinned by a range of commissioned research studies, three of which focused on the forensic analysis and use of biological material in criminal investigations and prosecutions (Robertson 1992; Roberts and Willmore 1993; Steventon 1993). The Commission made several important recommendations regarding police uses of DNA, the most important of which was that swabs taken from the mouth should be reclassified as non-intimate.[3] The Commission advised that:

DNA profiling is now so powerful a diagnostic technique and so helpful in establishing guilt or innocence, we believe that it is proper and desirable to allow the police to take non-intimate samples (e.g. saliva, plucked hair etc) without consent from all those arrested for serious criminal offences, whether or not DNA is relevant to the particular offence. (1993: 16)

This recommendation contains three important elements: the first is that the police should be allowed to take certain reclassified non-intimate samples without consent; the second is that the police be empowered to obtain such samples in instances of 'serious criminal offences' – although it was further suggested that 'as soon as resources, with or without advances in technology, permit, we recommend that the category of serious arrestable offences be extended to include, for this purpose only, assault and burglary' (The Royal Commission 1993: 15); and the third is that the police be allowed to obtain a non-intimate sample regardless of its relevance to the investigation in question. This marks a significant shift from the sampling provisions implemented by PACE and must be seen as the first recommendation supporting the collection of DNA for the purposes of databasing rather than simply for individual police casework. In making these recommendations the Royal Commission acknowledged that changes in the law on the collection and storage of samples were necessary 'so that, in any subsequent investigation where the identity of the offender is unknown but DNA evidence comes to light, that evidence can be checked against the samples in a data base' (1993: 15).[4]

It is against this background that the construction of the NDNAD was formulated and has progressed. Throughout the development of the legislation supporting the database there has been, and remains, a constant tension between the desire of successive governments to maximise the powers of the police to obtain and use bodily samples taken from suspects during investigations, and with a recognition that such sampling is restricted by legal and normative understandings of bodily integrity. For instance, the 1987 report by Touche Ross recommended that 'information about arrestees should be recorded in greater detail so that information from DNA profiles in the future can be compared' (1987, para 1.10, emphasis added). In fact, it wasn't until 16 years later, in 2003, that the police were granted such powers to take samples and retain profiles from arrestees. Yet in the intervening years, an important series of legislative changes has continually expanded the scope of the police to populate the database. It is an expansion that is easily characterised by the grammar of 'function' or 'control creep' which describes how a government's programme of technological intervention into social life is gradually, incrementally, but deliberately, increased over time:

> This control creep is an artefact of how we as a society construct and react to our collective and individual fears about the dangers that we believe assail us, and the problems we face in manufacturing a sense of security in relation to them. To date, the central social problem around which such concerns have gravitated is crime and the fear of being a victim of crime. (Innes 2001: 2.2)

Notions of civil security and a fear of crime have been central to constructing the NDNAD in its current form and have underpinned each stage of legislative activity by government.

While the legislative history we are describing does demonstrate a degree of function creep, it also shows a more fractured development in which change is driven less by an overall dogmatism and more by an ongoing series of pragmatic adjustments and corrections. It is fruitful to think of such change as underpinned by alterations in the discourses which have constructed and produced the NDNAD, and the population of individuals to which it is applied, as legitimate 'objects'. In other words, as Foucault notes, objects which have appeared because of changes in discursive relations, relations 'established between institutions, economic and social processes, behavioural patterns, systems of norms, techniques, types of classification, modes of characterization' (Foucault 1972: 45). The development of the NDNAD cannot be seen as independent of such relations since its very existence and expansion rely upon changes in discourses concerned with the social management of crime and criminality. Legislation is one element of an imbricated set of discourses – in policing, in public sector management, in forensic science – which together combine to produce and sustain both social conceptions of, and practical solutions to crime. To think of legislative development in this way is to think of change impelled through dynamic inter-relationships across a number of sites and, as we explore below, explains its rather stuttering and fragmented progression.

Finding a subject: making the NDNAD in law

When the government enacted the Criminal Justice and Public Order

Act (CJPOA) 1994, which was directly influenced by the 1993 Royal Commission, it extended police powers in two central ways: first, by affording the police greater powers to obtain and retain CJ samples, and second, by making specific provisions for the speculative searching of the profiles derived from such samples. In relation to the first, a far reaching aspect of the CJPOA was the new framework it created for the police administration of DNA sample collection: in line with the Royal Commission's recommendation, the CJPOA redefined mouth samples as non-intimate and empowered the police to take them without consent. Yet the CJPOA amendments to PACE went beyond the suggestions of the Royal Commission by permitting non-intimate samples to be taken without consent in connection with the investigation of any 'recordable offence' (as opposed to 'serious offence'). The reason for this was to widen the 'pool' of criminal suspects from which CJ samples could be taken and, as a result, when the NDNAD went live on 10 April 1995 it was quickly populated with a large number of CJ profiles taken from all those charged with, or convicted of, a recordable offence – 39,712 CJ profiles, as well as 2881 crime scene profiles, were added in 1995/6 (for a full statistical breakdown of annual profile inclusion by the FSS see: the NDNAD Annual Report 2002–03). No data exist to assess the volume of profiles that were held by the police prior to 1995 although they are assumed to be of significant number. As specified by the CJPOA, CJ samples and profiles obtained from those suspects subsequently not convicted of a recordable offence were subject to removal from the NDNAD.

Following the CJPOA two further pieces of legislation were enacted to enhance new police powers to sample and database samples and profiles. The first, the Criminal Procedure and Investigations Act (1996) (Section 64), widened the power of the police to speculatively search samples and profiles taken from those who were arrested, charged or informed they would be reported for a recordable offence. The Act extended the power of the police to search profiles obtained across the whole of the UK (including Scotland, Northern Ireland, Jersey, Guernsey and the Isle of Man). In 1996 Scottish forces submitted samples and profiles directly to the FSS for inclusion on the NDNAD but have since established their own database (see Johnson and Williams 2004). At the time of writing, there is no routine incorporation of samples or profiles into the NDNAD from Northern Ireland (the Forensic Science Northern Ireland do not possess the required accreditation to submit profiles to the NDNAD).

A second piece of legislation, the Criminal Evidence (Amendment)

Act 1997, extended the power of the police to take non-intimate samples without consent from a limited category of prisoners convicted before the CJPOA took effect. The legislation was designed to allow the police to collect DNA samples from those convicted of sex offences prior to 1994 to ensure their subsequent inclusion on the database. The introduction of retrospective sampling powers was justified by government because of the serious nature of the offences under consideration.

However, the most significant piece of legislation since the CJPOA has been the Criminal Justice and Police Act (CJPA) 2001 which extended the powers of the police to retain and speculatively search the samples and profiles of those not convicted of a recordable offence. It is worth considering the background to the CJPA extension of police powers in some detail since it is important to understanding how change has been driven by a range of stakeholders operating at a number of social sites. One important aspect to this change was the joint failure of the police and the FSS to ensure the systematic removal of profiles from the NDNAD taken from those who were subsequently never convicted of criminal offences. A report by Her Majesty's Inspectorate of Constabulary in 2000 (HMIC 2000: 16–18) recognised that a large number of samples and profiles – estimated at 50,000 but acknowledged to be perhaps higher – was currently being held on the NDNAD unlawfully. These samples, taken from suspects who were later not prosecuted or whose prosecutions failed, should have been destroyed and the profiles obtained from them removed from the NDNAD. When the NDNAD subsequently produced matches between CJ profiles that should have been removed (i.e. profiles of unconvicted persons) and newly entered crime scene profiles, this proved highly problematic for police investigations and prosecutions.

The practical failure in record keeping by the Custodian of the NDNAD generated a considerable debate regarding the permissible uses of illegally held intelligence by the police and the lawful admission of evidence derived from such intelligence in court. Importantly, the issue framed a consideration of the 'balance' of rights and powers instantiated through the tripartite relationship between the police (and their duty to exploit available intelligence to detect criminal suspects), the Crown Prosecution Service (and their responsibility to utilise available evidence to prosecute suspects), and individual subjects (and their legal rights during the process of police investigation and criminal prosecution). A good example of this can be seen in the contestations made in one criminal case, R *v*

B, where the original prosecution relied on DNA evidence obtained using an illegally retained CJ profile. The background to R *v* B was the rape and assault of a 66 year old woman in her London home on 23 January 1997. On 20 March 1997 the FSS produced DNA profiles from semen found on two swabs taken from the woman which were subsequently loaded onto the NDNAD on 15 April. On 4 January 1998, 'B' was arrested in respect of an offence of burglary and a DNA sample was taken from him. The sample was received by the FSS for profiling on 6 January but not loaded onto the NDNAD until 23 September, one month after 'B' had been acquitted of charges of burglary. Under the provisions of the CJPOA, because 'B' had been acquitted, the profile should not have been included on the database. However, when it was loaded, it matched the profile obtained from the swabs taken from the rape victim 20 months earlier.

When 'B' was arrested for rape following police receipt of the DNA intelligence match, a criminal prosecution followed. In court, the trial judge ruled that, because the case rested on an initial detection by the police obtained using an illegally held sample and profile, the subsequent DNA evidence was inadmissible. The Attorney General contested this ruling in the Court of Appeal on 26 May 2000. The Court of Appeal considered the legislative framework for the retention and use of DNA samples, recommending 'a balance between the importance of investigating serious crime and convicting those who have committed serious crimes on the one hand and the rights and interests of the citizens on the other' (R *v* B 2000). Determining that the evidence submitted in R *v* B was based on an 'impermissible link' the court stated that:

It would have been perfectly possible for Parliament to conclude that the fight against crime was so important that there should be no restriction on the use of DNA samples, so that where such samples were lawfully obtained by the Police the information derived from them could be retained on a database for all purposes ... [t]he [legislation] expressly and without qualification forbids the use of the sample which is required to be destroyed either in evidence or for the purposes of investigation. (R *v* B 2000)

The subsequent judgment of the House of Lords, who deemed the Court of Appeal ruling 'contrary to good sense', contended that such an 'austere' interpretation of the legislation unnecessarily limited the power of the police to investigate, and the Crown Prosecution Service to prosecute, an individual where compelling evidence was available. The House of Lords judgment coincided with the recommendation from HMIC that 'in the general interest of crime detection and reduction' it was time to 'revisit the legislation to consider whether all CJ samples, provided they have been obtained in accordance with PACE, should be retained on the NDNAD to provide a useful source of intelligence to aid future investigations' (HMIC 2000: 18).

The extension of police powers afforded by the CJPA was not driven simply by rectifying the problems highlighted by cases such as R v B. What such cases allowed was a convenient platform for the realisation of a more general government policy ambition first expressed during 2000. When the then Prime Minister Tony Blair 'hailed an acceleration in the high-tech drive against crime, with the major expansion of the police DNA database used to hunt down criminals', he made a firm commitment to utilise this 'vital weapon in the law enforcement arsenal' by creating, by 2004, a database containing '3 million suspect samples – virtually the entire criminally active population' (Home Office Announcement 269/2000). As we argued in Chapter 2, the idea of recording the details of a discernable criminal population or a population of 'suspects' is certainly not new. Yet the rhetoric of an 'active criminal population', permanently captured on the NDNAD, and comprising some three million 'suspect samples', was a spectacular proposal given the legislative framework in place for obtaining and databasing samples. In 2000 the database held 940,000 CJ samples and, even with increased funding to facilitate police to obtain and submit a greater volume of samples, a database of three million 'suspects' by 2004, under the existing legislative framework created by the CJPOA, would have been impossible.

The discursive construction of the 'active criminal population' as a distinct social body, including anyone who had been charged with but not necessarily convicted of a recordable offence, was crucial in legitimating the expansion of the database. While the extension of legal powers to the police often appears as a reactive solution to established social problems – because it is presented as a method of combating pre-identified crime issues – the formulation of legislation is actively implicated in the social construction of cultural representations of both crime and criminal groups. This is nowhere more apparent than in the use of the term 'active criminal population' because it interpellates a specific population of individuals which requires particular technologies of management and control. The changing nomenclature of the population captured on the NDNAD – it was originally described by the FSS as a 'suspect database' – is not mere semantics; rather it is an element of the changing discursive relations through which individuals are conceived, strategies are formulated, and practices are enacted. In this sense, the discursive construction of the 'active criminal' establishes the identity of a group of individuals for the purposes of policing them; as Judith Butler argues, its 'purpose is to indicate and establish a subject in subjection' (1997: 37). As such, therefore, the conception of this population was central to the CJPA which allows for the indefinite retention of DNA samples on the NDNAD, obtained from suspects not convicted or cautioned for a crime, along with those 50,000+ samples that were currently held illegally.

The end of innocence: extending NDNAD inclusion

The enactment of the Criminal Justice Act (CJA) 2003 further extended the powers of the police to obtain non-intimate CJ samples without the consent from any person in police detention following their arrest for a recordable offence. The Act, which grants the police powers to sample, profile and database individuals arrested but not subsequently charged or convicted in connection with a recordable offence, adds a new 'category' of person to the database: the one-time suspect who may never have been charged with a recordable offence and has no criminal record. The number of such individuals is considerable. The Home Office calculates that 300,000 individuals are arrested each year in connection with a recordable offence but not subsequently charged. This does not mean an increase of 300,000 additional profiles year-on-year to the NDNAD – since a proportion of those arrested will have been sampled and profiled at the time of a previous arrest – but the potential effect of the CJA on the size of the database is nevertheless significant.

The CJA is the first piece of legislation relating to the NDNAD to have generated substantial parliamentary debate. In October 2003, the House of Lords rejected a government amendment to the Criminal Justice Bill proposing the extension of police powers to retain non-intimate samples from arrestees. The Minister of State, Baroness Scotland, told the House of Lords that taking DNA samples at the point of arrest would 'allow more crimes to be resolved at an earlier stage' because the police could 'prevent persons who may have previously come into contact with the criminal justice system from evading justice by giving the police a false identity' (Hansard, House of Lords, 29 October 2003). She also argued that retaining these samples was justified by their potential usefulness in future investigations, not least in cases involving the arrest of juveniles:

> Many young people who may be arrested as juveniles are not charged and may never go on to commit an offence. However, it is difficult for the police to distinguish between those who may or may not commit a crime in the future. It is, therefore, a sensible precaution to retain DNA profiles as a norm. (Baroness Scotland, Hansard, House of Lords, 29 October 2003)

This statement gives a clear indication of the government's intention to capture on the NDNAD an even more broadly defined potentially active criminal population. It is this objective of the Act, to database and retain samples for the future identification of potential offenders, rather than the taking of samples for the purpose of identity verification, which has been most disputed. This is a distinction which the Lords recognised to be significant: 'There are two principles here: the propriety of taking fingerprints [and samples] from a person who has been arrested but not charged and the decision to add that information to a database' (Hansard, House of Lords, 29 October 2003). The emphasis on retaining records from innocent individuals who have never been formally charged with an offence for use in future investigations is a significant shift in English law. This change relies upon judgments about who should be subject to the type of speculative searching which the database allows. As Beyleveld (1997) has argued, such a question is not distinctive of police uses of DNA but reflects well-established disputes about the purpose of the criminal justice system and the normative relationship between an individual and society. Nevertheless, it is the technological capabilities of DNA which have driven changes in that normative relationship and extended police powers.

In most European jurisdictions, as Guillén (2000) argues, concerns about the potential of offender recidivism have been the major determinant of the regulations governing DNA retention. In other words, it is particular types of offenders, and the risks they pose, which are subject to this form of criminal administration. While the majority of European nations have created forensic DNA databases, there remains a focus on recording specific offenders or individuals who have committed certain crimes. Many European nations limit the types of offences for which the police can obtain compulsory samples from suspects: for example, in Austria police can only collect DNA from certain suspects of 'severe' crimes (such as crimes against the person) and in Finland and The Netherlands sampling is delimited to crimes which attract specific terms of imprisonment as a punishment (in Finland six months, in The Netherlands four years). There are a plethora of legislative arrangements governing the sampling and databasing of DNA taken from suspects across Europe and the rest of the world, but what such differences show is that decisions regarding who should be subject to DNA databasing are based on conceptions of the potential of certain individuals to reoffend.

As Michel Foucault (1977) argued, the processes of detecting, demarking and managing populations of 'dangerous subjects' are implicitly linked. In other words, technologies designed to control specific individuals actively shape conceptions about 'who' and 'what' such people are and the risks they pose. As we argued above, the establishment of the NDNAD has itself relied upon a reconfiguration of discourses on criminality. On the one hand, a normative discourse on the dangers posed by the possibility of recidivist offenders has been used to justify the inclusion of certain individuals on the database. An example of this can be seen in the enactment of the Criminal Evidence (Amendment) Act (CEAA) 1997 which empowered the police to obtain DNA samples from a range of individuals who were already convicted (or held under the Mental Health Act) prior to the CJPOA and who were still incarcerated. The CEAA served to retrospectively extend powers granted under the CJPOA so that a number of prisoners – namely those convicted of violent or sexual offences – could be sampled and entered onto the NDNAD. The justification for these retrospective powers, to 'mop up' those convicted of sexual or violent offences prior to 1994, was that such offenders often have a history of recidivism and a high chance of reoffending after release; or, as Ian Brownlee puts it, 'the taking and recording of DNA samples was specifically intended to operate as a form of "biological tagging" of sex offenders for preventative as well as investigative purposes' (1998: 416). The CEAA enabled a 'mopping up' exercise which comprised the collection of 13,000 samples from prisoners and mentally disordered offenders.

On the other hand, the development of the NDNAD to hold the entire population of 'known suspect offenders' has relied upon another change in discourses about criminality, criminal careers, and offender behaviour. In contrast to the mopping up of 'serious' offenders is the inclusion of all arrestees on the NDNAD regardless of the type of offence for which they were suspected. Including such persons on the database is clearly based on notions that those who come to the attention of the police are worthy of attention in the future. As Helena Kennedy, chair of the Human Genetics Commission, argues: 'Underlying our new hoarding of DNA seems to be the cynical belief that those suspected of a crime are probably guilty, even if acquitted, and likely to be involved in further offending' (2004: 270). In the justifications provided by government for arrestee retention the language of 'innocence' has disappeared completely: such individuals are 'one time suspects' rather than innocent individuals who were never subject to criminal charges. A consequence of the NDNAD, therefore, is that it has come to act as both a reason and justification for the need to subject all arrestees to further police surveillance.

As an example of this, the Home Office and police regularly offer the NDNAD 'success' at detecting crimes using DNA profiles retained from those with no previous conviction as a justification for such retention: they argue that retaining all the samples from those charged with an offence, but not subsequently convicted, has led to the detection of 6,280 offences, including '53 murders, 33 attempted murders, 94 rapes, 38 sexual offences, 63 aggravated burglaries and 56 [for] the supply of controlled drugs' (NDNAD Annual Report 2004: 6). While these statistics are contentious for a number of reasons – not least because they do not show how many of the crimes were detected using DNA intelligence solely – their deployment is crucial in reiterating the idea that those who were once the subject of police suspicion are potential, even likely, future offenders. While this may be normative in western societies in relation to the convicted population, or even those charged with serious offences, the shift to including any person arrested for any offence in such a category is significant.

While many jurisdictions use the distinction between 'serious' and 'minor' offences for the purpose of adjudicating which persons will be subject to databasing, some commentators have argued that, regardless of the offence, the actual existence of *any* archive which is speculatively searched by the police raises the most serious ethical concerns. Bereano (1992), for example, argues that limiting the use of DNA to crime scene collection and individual casework (where a DNA sample is taken from an individual already suspected of a crime in order to provide a comparison with crime scene material) is ethically viable because it can be justified as a breach of privacy in relation to each legitimate investigation. However, he also argues the databasing of a permanent set of records used for 'fishing expeditions' to find suspects erodes this aspect of civil liberty. As we argued earlier, this reflects a more general concern that speculative searching on the NDNAD is a mechanism of surveillance which is being used to continually monitor individuals. It is present in regular assertions (predominantly from human rights and civil liberties groups) that the NDNAD contributes to the creation of a 'suspect society', whereby certain individuals are deemed to be suspects and not citizens (see Williams and Johnson 2004, for a discussion of the issue of surveillance).

Despite continual expressions of concern about the growth and impact of state surveillance it is rare to find arguments like Bereano's. Most critical commentators in the UK support at least some retention of DNA on police databases for ensuring public safety and the detection of future offences. Genewatch UK, for instance, who have been highly critical of the expanded inclusion regime of the NDNAD have argued in favour of the retention of DNA profiles from those charged, but not convicted, of sexual or violent offences. While Genewatch (2005: 9) would argue that '[k]eeping innocent people on the database effectively means treating them as criminals' and that this practice 'undermines the principle of "innocent until proven guilty"', they offer no justification for the distinction they themselves make between retaining DNA samples from those who were one time suspects of certain crimes. If, as Genewatch note, the principle of 'innocent until proven guilty' is undermined by inclusion on the database, because this constitutes a form of suspicion, then surely this principle must be applied universally?

Yet, the distinction which Genewatch makes between certain types of offences, in order to justify the retention of specific individuals on the NDNAD, utilises the same conceptual apparatus that the government deploys to justify the inclusion of all those arrested for recordable offences: it is a distinction based on categories of suspects. This categorical differentiation between persons is used to argue for a legitimate reduction in privacy rights for specific individuals. Prior to changes created by the CJPA, such a distinction was formulated in relation to conviction – that is, those convicted of recordable offences were subject to reduced privacy rights. The CJA 2003 has reformulated the distinction so that suspicion is a sufficient basis to curtail the right to privacy. The outcome of this change is the instantiation of a new category of individuals held on the NDNAD – the one time arrested or charged suspect.

Contesting the law: privacy, discrimination and the Human Rights Act

The expanded retention regime enabled by the CJPA 2001 (subsequently extended by the CJA 2003) has been challenged in the UK's courts. This challenge, which is essentially concerned to contend the legitimacy of the categorisations of persons captured by the NDNAD as either 'suspects' or 'active criminals', has utilised the Human Rights Act 1998. This act grants courts in England and Wales the power to rule on whether the actions of public authorities (including the police) are in compliance with the articles and principles of the European Convention on Human Rights (ECHR). The ECHR has itself been central to European jurisprudence since its inception in Rome in 1950 and, with its subsequent five 'protocol' amendments made between 1952 and 1966, has had far reaching impacts on a number of relevant jurisdictions. The ECHR has been the basis for an important case, which has now been heard on three occasions by the Courts of England and Wales (R v Marper & 'S' 2002a, 2002b, 2004), in which the appellants have used Articles 8 and 14 of the convention to challenge the legitimacy of the legislation governing DNA retention.

Article 8 (1) of the ECHR states that: 'everyone has the right to respect for his private and family life, his home and his correspondence'. Necessarily this is characterised as a 'qualified right' – a right whose exercise has to be balanced against the rights of others or the interests of society in general (other qualified rights are the 'right to freedom of expression'; the 'right to freedom of assembly'; and the 'right to the peaceful enjoyment of possessions'). The nature of the qualification is described in Article 8 (2) which states that:

> There shall be no interference by a public authority with the exercise of this right except such as is in accordance with the law and is necessary in a democratic society in the interests of national security, public safety or the economic well-being of the country, for the prevention of disorder or crime, for the protection of health or morals, or for the protection of the rights and freedoms of others.

While it is generally recognised that 'a range of policing actions impinge upon Article 8 including the interception of communications, surveillance, the storage and retention of DNA, fingerprints and communications data, and search and seizure' (Taylor 2003: 45), the appellants in R *v* Marper & 'S' claim that the retention of DNA from unconvicted individuals is not a justifiable interference.

This case concerns the retention of DNA samples and profiles of two individuals, one a 12 year old boy, who were once charged with recordable offences but not subsequently convicted. The Chief Constable of South Yorkshire Police, exercising powers afforded by the CJPA 2001, refused a request by the appellants to have their samples and fingerprints destroyed following their discharge. The resulting civil case was brought first to the High Court in 2002, then subsequently to the Court of Appeal in 2002, and last heard in June 2004 in the House of Lords (the Court of final appeal for the UK). In all three instances the appellants' case has been dismissed.

The case is specifically concerned with the privacy issues raised by the *retention* of DNA samples and profiles by the police and not with the conditions under which they were taken. This is an important distinction since it precludes any interrogation of the legitimacy of the legislation which allows the police to breach bodily integrity to obtain non-consensual samples without consent. It seems generally accepted in UK jurisprudence that the police should have the right to obtain DNA samples for comparison on the NDNAD at the point of charging an individual, whether or not there exists evidence relevant DNA to the investigation of the offence for which the individual is being charged. However, the case shows that the Convention is clearly subject to jurisprudential interpretation in relation to the retention and subsequent use of such samples and derived profiles. For instance, Article 8 (2) states that any breach of the right to respect for private and family life must be 'in accordance with the law' and that it any interference should be 'necessary in a democratic country'. The appellants in R *v* Marper & 'S' contend that there is no such necessity for the retention of the samples and profiles of the unconvicted and that, on those grounds, the law is incompatible with Article 8 (1). In the absence of such necessity, they assert, the powers accorded to the police by the CJPA 2001 to retain samples and profiles subsequent to criminal acquittal are not proportionate to the legitimate aim of detecting and preventing crime.[5]

When considering the proportionality of any particular policing action there are a number of general factors which the courts take into account:

- any action must not restrict the right in question so much that it 'impairs its essence';

- the action has to be determined in the context of the individual case as a whole;
- insofar as the interference is discretionary, decision making must be considered and not arbitrary;
- the nature and severity of any potential harm to the individual whose rights have been interfered with must be considered; and
- the existence of less restrictive or less intrusive alternatives will have to have been considered.

For Feldman (2002) these considerations mean having to balance the extent of the interference against the reasons for interfering – not balancing the right against the interference. However, inevitably and necessarily, the actual substantive issues raised in any consideration draw upon the context, circumstances and the significance of the categorical identities of the appellants who are making the case. Since the police do not possess the power to collect and retain the DNA samples of the entire population the question in judicial hearings has been framed as: is the indefinite retention of DNA samples and the indefinite speculative searching of profiles taken from individuals who were once subject to criminal charges a proportionate breach of their right to privacy under Article 8 of the ECHR? In asking this question in R *v* Marper & 'S' a specific category of person has been invoked – the 'charged suspect' – and factual and normative disputes about this category of person have been fundamental to the challenges and decisions made in the case.

For instance, the appellants assert that the retention of their DNA samples and profiles unfairly discriminates against their entitlement to privacy and therefore contravenes their right to fair and equal treatment outlined by Article 14 of the ECHR.[6] In other words, that in allowing the police the power to retain their DNA, the legislation creates a discriminatory distinction between the appellants (as once charged but unconvicted) and the larger unconvicted population. It is the legitimacy of this distinction which has been the foundation on which all three judicial rulings in this case have been based. While each ruling has recognised that the CJPA 2001 instantiates a particular category of person, to which a particular forensic regime subsequently has been applied, none of the judges have accepted that Article 14 of the ECHR has been breached. This is significant given that it represents a break from normative considerations of the balance between the public good and individual rights which is usually formulated as the balance between the good of the *innocent* collective versus the rights of a legitimately *suspected* individual.

In this sense, deliberations of proportionality are concerned with whether the consequences of a policing measure are adverse to the suspected individual to the extent that they outweigh the benefits derivable for the collective.[7] Insofar as DNA profile comparison may serve to exonerate as well as incriminate, the act of taking a DNA sample from a legitimate suspect and generating a profile from it during the course of a specific investigation may be generally accepted as a proportionate response to the necessity to investigate crime. Furthermore, in considering the arrangements for retaining fingerprints and samples from the *convicted* population of England and Wales the answer to the question of proportionality has also been a positive one, because of the generally accepted distinction between the categories of 'proven guilty' and 'innocent' individuals. However, since the 2001 legislation now allows for the retention of samples and profiles from those who, hitherto, would have been (like the rest of the unconvicted population) exempt from such retention, the question of balance is somewhat altered. This is because the question of balance does not concern guilt versus innocence but, rather, persons where police suspicion of involvement in a recordable offence was once deemed sufficient to authorise charges being laid against them versus those never suspected of (or at least never charged with) involvement in a recordable offence.

There has been no clear justification in England and Wales for the retention and use of DNA profiles and samples obtained from innocent ex-suspects. Whereas the Lord Chief Justice, in his consideration of R *v* Marper & 'S' (2002b), ruled that it is legitimate to distinguish those who have been subject to sampling (because they have been legitimately charged with a recordable offence) and those who have not, he provided no assessment of the delivery of possible benefits to both policing and the social good. Although the police may derive a further 'convenience' from the establishment of a wide retention regime, it is questionable whether social, financial or administrative benefits are sufficiently great to justify the extension of powers without extended consideration and justification about the effects on individuals who have been subjected to different agencies and stages of the criminal justice process. Critics of the legislation claim that the profiles and samples of these unconvicted individuals are retained on the basis that such persons are deemed to be 'less innocent' than the general population who have never been subject to arrest or charge. As Lord Justice Sedley argued: 'Not all unconvicted people, in other words, are equal from a policing point of view, even though they are from a legal one; and among those who have been charged but not convicted it is especially so' (R *v* Marper & 'S' 2002b: 20). However, the criticism of this view, as one member of the House of Lords prosaically put it, is that it relies upon an illegitimate distinction between 'the guilty who have been convicted of offences, the not guilty, and the probably dodgy' (The Lord Bishop of Worcester, Hansard, House of Lords, 29 October 2003).

In the most recent consideration of R *v* Marper & 'S' the Appellate Committee of the House of Lords did not reach a consensus on whether the retention of DNA samples and profiles constituted an intrusion of privacy under Article 8 (1) of the Convention. Whereas, as stated above, the Lord Chief Justice of England and Wales deemed it an intrusion, albeit a 'small' one, the House of Lords demurred from this ruling. However, Baroness Hale strongly argued that both the taking of samples and profiles and their subsequent retention most certainly do contravene Article 8 (1). Her argument to justify this intrusion of privacy was:

> The whole community, as well as the individuals whose samples are collected, benefits from there being as large a database as it is possible to have. The present system is designed to allow the collection of as many samples as possible and to retain as much as possible of what it has. The benefit to the aims of accurate and efficient law enforcement is thereby enhanced. (R *v* Marper & 'S' 2004: para 78)

This justification of recognised intrusiveness distinguishes between the 'whole community' and the group of individuals who have been subject to sampling. Yet the distinction is blurred when suspects are 'returned' to the community without having been convicted of an offence (and, since the CJA 2003, may not have been charged). If the retention of their DNA is beneficial to law enforcement because it expands the database, is the logical conclusion to such a view that the most effective database would be a universal one? Yet there seems no enthusiasm for the establishment of a population-wide forensic DNA database in England and Wales, even among those who currently support the establishment of an 'Identity Register' which will underpin the planned introduction of identity cards some time in the next decade. This lack of enthusiasm contrasts with a lack of explanation or justification from government about the significant shift in English law to allow for the retention and use of samples of the innocent, save that these individuals are now conceived as differentiated from the 'innocent population' by virtue of having been one time suspects of the police.

Conclusion: the reconfigured criminal body

The systematic extensions of the legal powers affording the police the capacity to sample, store and speculatively search the DNA profiles of an increasingly heterogeneous group of 'suspects' have produced a significant shift in the discursive construction of both the individual and social criminal body. The legislation underpinning DNA sampling has reframed the human body in law and redrawn its intimate boundaries. Just as parliamentary legislation in the nineteenth century 'invented' the mouth as a legal bodily object for the application of medical techniques (Nettleton 1994), so too have the amendments to PACE constructed the mouth as a particular bodily orifice suitable for subjection to police invasion and inspection. Whereas prior to 1994 the mouth was accorded the status of intimate in law, in line with other intimate bodily orifices such as the anus and vagina, legislators have reconceived the mouth as an area deemed suitable for compulsory investigation. Such a shift has been achieved through an asserted campaign by government to 'de-intimatise' the mouth and represent the practice of mouth swabbing as non-invasive and harmless. From pictures of the Prime Minister undergoing a buccal swab to statements by the Home Office that such a procedure requires 'minimum' invasion, the mouth has ceased to be deemed a bodily area in need of the protections afforded to other orifices or openings. This discursive reconstruction of the body has been impelled by the technological development of DNA profiling but has also facilitated the increasing investigative use of forensic DNA by maximising the sampling opportunities of the police.

If the discursive construction of the NDNAD has reconceived the individual body it has also produced effects upon conceptions of the social body. The capacity of DNA databases to capture a discrete population of individuals for the purpose of future criminal detection has significantly altered ideas about the 'types' of persons who comprise such a population. While, as we argued in Chapter 2, the existence of conceptions about criminal populations and attempts to document them have a long history, the NDNAD has created significant changes to such conceptions and practices. Like other technologies before it, the application of DNA profiling has been complicit in actively shaping the social populations to which it is applied. What is ultimately significant about the NDNAD is that it has delimited an 'active suspect criminal population' currently comprising 5 per cent of the population of the UK. This group comprises the most heterogeneous mix of persons ever recorded in a central criminal archive: from convicted offenders, to one time suspects, to volunteers. The NDNAD has actively invented this new criminal population, made it 'real', and imbued it with specific properties to distinguish it from the rest of the 'community'. The legislative development which this chapter has traced is a development of an instrument to demark and record this new social body.

As Nikolas Rose argues, contemporary techniques of crime management 'target offenders as an aggregate; they do not aim to rehabilitate' (1999: 236). The practical application of crime management, as we argued earlier in this book, is concerned to define, diagnose, and contain danger and risk. The NDNAD is an exemplar of this process in its ability to hold the genetic data of any potentially dangerous subject for the purposes of subsequent detection and capture. What is so significant about the individuals included in this aggregate is that their qualification for inclusion is no longer based on any judicial differentiation between innocence and guilt; inclusion on the NDNAD is not subject to adjudication by due criminal justice process but rather by police suspicion. For this reason, the legislative shifts in the UK substantiate Gerlach's (2004) observation that DNA technologies have impacted upon individual liberty by enabling judgments to be made about persons prior to judicial consideration. This is the essence of the contestations made in R *v* Marper & 'S', where the appellants claim that the retention of their DNA samples and profiles categorises them in a way which unjustifiably discriminates them from the population at large. While the courts have not recognised the legislation as the basis for discrimination they have conceded that it breaches, with justification, an individual's right to privacy as formulated by the ECHR. The justification most often provided by the courts and by government for this invasion is that it is outweighed by the contribution of the NDNAD to both detect and reduce crime. Yet many claims for the overall effectiveness of the database remain contested and in the next chapter we consider the evidence available to support claims made in favour of extensions in its inclusion regime.

Notes

1 'A procedure has been developed to facilitate research into the storage and manipulation of the results of DNA analysis by computer. In conjunction with Foster and Freeman Limited a video camera has been coupled to a microcomputer and software produced that allows the user to store data

effectively. The software also allows additional data to be compared with that already held and, in addition, frequencies of the incidence and chance co-migration of bands can be obtained. The system is interactive and should be very 'user friendly' in its final form' (Home Office 1988: 11).

2 An earlier consideration of the extent to which the police should be enabled to obtain DNA samples was undertaken by the Scottish Law Commission in 1989. In Scotland, DNA profiling had already been successfully used in a number of criminal prosecutions (see, CM 572, 1989: 2), and was also being utilised to settle paternity disputes in civil hearings. In the context of criminal investigations the Scottish Law Commission affirmed the recommendation from the Home Affairs Select Committee that courts should be empowered to order non-consensual blood testing (in Scotland, courts were already able to issue warrants affording the police the power to obtain intimate samples without consent). Yet while the Scottish Law Commission supported the collection of samples from certain suspects under particular conditions they also argued for restrictions on police powers. For instance, the Commission recommended that the police should not be given powers to take samples without consent where this 'involves going inside a person's body' (CM 572, 1989: 12). They recommended what they described as a 'halfway' approach – between fingerprinting (which they recognised as non-invasive) and blood sampling – to enable the police to obtain samples from plucked hair or swabs from external parts of the body. They argued that 'any invasion of bodily integrity in the taking of samples of the type we are considering is minimal. This is not to say that the taking of a sample from a person's body is a matter to be treated lightly. It is most certainly not. But it must be kept in perspective' (CM 572, 1989: 10).

3 It is important to recognise that the legislative framework which has since been developed to enable non-consensual CJ sampling in England and Wales was, at the end of the 1980s, already in place in Northern Ireland. A crucial difference in the legislative provision for sampling in Northern Ireland, and in contrast to the rest of the UK, was the designation of samples obtained from a swab inside the mouth, or saliva samples, as 'non-intimate' (Police and Criminal Evidence [Northern Ireland] Order 1989). This procedure, which allowed a 'buccal scrape' to be used to obtain epithelial cells from inside the mouth, was considered as intimate in England and Wales.

4 The Commission recommended the establishment of two data sets: one set of samples and profiles retained from those convicted, to be used for future identification; and a frequency data set, comprising only numerical data from both the convicted and unconvicted, to be held on a separate database, overseen by an independent body, and to be used for statistical assessment but not directly for the further investigation of crime.

5 While 'proportionality' is not a term found in the text of the ECHR, it has become a major resource for the formulation of arguments and

judgments concerning the police uses of DNA in the light of the ECHR. Proportionality, as the Lord Chief Justice stated in his judgement of R *v* Marper & 'S' (2002b), is usually absorbed by the consideration of 'balance' which the court is asked to make; that is, to judge an appropriate balance between an individual right and a collective or social good. Often in British jurisprudence a distinction is made between a 'balancing test' and a 'necessity test'. To judge necessity a court deliberates the possibility that the objective under consideration (in this case, the future prevention and detection of crime made possible by the NDNAD) could be met using different and less intrusive means. In R *v* Marper & 'S' the necessity test has been contended by arguing that the current 'blanket policy' of the police in retaining all samples and profiles of those once charged with, but not subsequently convicted of, a recordable offence is incompatible with the actual wording of the legislative provision in PACE which states that the police *may* retain samples and profiles. The appellants have argued that the intrusiveness created by the retention of samples and profiles, should there be a proven necessity for such a practice in particular instances, would be reduced by a case-by-case consideration of retention. This has been consistently ruled against on the grounds that such a situation would be potentially more intrusive because it would rely on the police making decisions about the 'character' of individual suspects. As Lord Wolf argued: 'It would be highly undesirable for members of the public to be treated differently on the basis of some scale of innocence derived by the police' (R *v* Marper & 'S' 2002b: 12).

6 Article 14 of the ECHR, which prohibits discrimination, states: 'The enjoyment of the rights and freedoms set forth in this Convention shall be secured without discrimination on any ground such as sex, race, colour, language, religion, political or other opinion, national or social origin, association with a national minority, property, birth or other status'.

7 There are certain problems in assessing proportionality in relation to the individual/society balance. As Lord Sedley notes 'proportionality [is] an issue which, with respect, I do not think can ever be absorbed in a simple balancing exercise as between the individual and the public (an exercise which in a majoritarian democracy the individual will always lose, and which the [European Convention on Human Rights] is there precisely to redress)' (R *v* Marper & 'S' 2002b: para 77).

Chapter 6

Using DNA effectively

Introduction

The continuous assertion by successive UK governments that DNA profiling and databasing are a vital weapon in the fight against crime has lead to significant amounts of fiscal investment across a range of laboratory and operational contexts. In this chapter we consider the nature and extent of this investment in DNA profiling and databasing. Specifically, we focus on the ways in which investment has been shaped by two imperatives which both seek to encourage 'effectiveness': first, a strong ethos of public sector audit culture and, second, a commitment to a particular form of 'intelligence-led policing'. We discuss the effects of these on political and operational efforts to encourage and evaluate the uses of DNA and describe how key stakeholders initially worked to shape the most significant form of investment – the DNA Expansion Programme. We also consider some of the available evidence on the effectiveness of police uses of DNA profiling and databasing and conclude by suggesting that existing methods of policing performance measurement are chronically ambiguous when applied to show the 'success' of complex socio-technical assemblages like the NDNAD.

Policing, forensic science and the new public management

When the then Minister of State, Lord Falconer, announced the introduction of the first Science and Technology Strategy for policing in 2003 he argued that because criminals had 'become more technologically aware' it was vital that the police service should be 'properly equipped to combat this new strain of criminals'. However, he emphasised that in equipping the police in this way it was vital that 'the tools they use are as effective and efficient as possible' (Hansard, 16 January 2003: Column WA56). This emphasis on making science and technology both effective and efficient is shorthand for describing the vast range of ways in which policing in the UK has become subject to forms of audit. In this section we describe the ways in which policing in general, and forensic science in particular, have become subject to a range of concepts, methods and practices designed to manage and measure their work.

All police forces in England and Wales are now subject to a common formal regime of local accounting, with additional elements of central control based on the establishment of 'norms, standards, benchmarks, performance indicators, quality controls and best practice standards, to monitor, measure and render calculable the[ir] performance' (Dean 1999: 165). First formulated as a concern with 'value for money', the application of the underlying economic rationality of the 'New Public Management' (NPM) approach to the 'modernisation' of the UK public sector from the early 1980s onwards has provided a methodology for the management of all government agencies. Described by several commentators (see, for example, Osborne and Gaebler 1992; Stewart and Walsh 1992; Zifcaf 1994; McLaughlin 2001, 2002), it has been characterised by Garland as having

> thematic and cultural coherence – the success of an exemplar, everywhere applied – rather than a strict logic or tight conceptual structure. It is in effect, a ragbag of techniques, models, analogies and recipes for action that are loosely bound up by their appeal to economic rationality … The economic rationality is, above all, a language for doing and representing. (Garland 2001: 190)

When applied to policing this framework has meant that police work has increasingly been understood as simply one of the many 'markets in services, provision and expertise' (Dean 1999: 161) that make up modern public sector organisations, albeit one of the later ones to have emerged following a series of efforts by successive governments.

The Home Office Circular 114 ('Manpower Effectiveness and Efficiency in the Police Service', 1983) provides a good early example of the emerging valorisation of concepts of 'economy', 'efficiency' and 'effectiveness' which later became central to the NPM and which were heavily promoted by the Audit Commission in the 1980s. The 'Three "E's"' were a way of shifting the focus of measurement and evaluation of organisational performance away from 'inputs' (as amounts of manpower, finance or other elements expended by units) to 'outputs' (as measures of artefacts produced by organisational activity) and to 'outcomes' (as measures of achieved desired organisational ends attributable to relevant outputs). Ten years later the White Paper on Police Reform (Home Office 1992), which informed the Police and Magistrates Courts Bill of 1994, was fully engaged with many, of what had become by then, well-established principles of the NPM. Despite its opposition to many of the recommendations of the Sheehey Report, ACPO contributed to this trend by their approval of six performance indicators which were included among the Audit Commission's suite of indicators in 1996–7. These were subsequently developed into a small number of national objectives in the National Policing Plan which established a 'Treasury based linkage between a set of performance targets and the revenue budgets for police forces' (Neyroud 2003: 580).

The endorsement by the Audit Commission of NPM and its 'ethos of business management, monetary measurement and value-for-money government' (Garland 2001: 116) has meant that both existing and proposed forms of police practice have increasingly become subject to its developing discursive framework. Accordingly the application of measures of economy, efficiency and effectiveness has been central to how various kinds of forensic support to criminal investigation have been interrogated and shaped within the police forces of England and Wales. In particular, they have underpinned efforts to arrive at a standardised way of representing and comparing the individual and collective performance of a variety of contributors within police forces and other agencies. In turn, such representations of actual and potential performance have been crucial both in determining what policy initiatives are supported and also in evaluating their 'success'. An early example of such influence can be seen in the report of the accountants commissioned by the Home Office to review the organisation of scientific support in police forces in the UK (Touche Ross 1987). This report serves as a crucial historical document because its economic 'style of reasoning' has provided a framework to which almost all subsequent studies have felt necessary to refer and, more often than not, endorse and adopt.

Touche Ross attributed the low levels of police confidence in forensic science in the mid-1980s to the failure of the Forensic Science

Service to respond to the needs of the police. They paid particular attention to the FSS's failure to produce an analysis of an increased volume of forensic submissions in a relatively timely fashion. The team of accountants proposed that the solution to this problem was the introduction of market mechanisms and the principle of 'direct charging' so that individual police forces would approach suppliers (including, but not exclusively, the FSS) to agree prices for the type and volume of forensic analysis they required. It was argued that such mechanisms would allow the police, as consumers, to directly affect the quality and quantity of the services they wanted in ways that were impossible when the FSS was directly controlled by the Home Office. Direct charging for forensic services to all police forces in England and Wales was introduced in 1991. In addition to the first introduction of a market (or quasi-market) for forensic services, the Touche Ross Report also included several other recommendations for changes in the organisation of scientific support within police forces. The introduction and further effects of these changes also provided a continuing focus of research for subsequent studies of the uses of forensic science within criminal investigations. Two particular recommendations were especially important.

The first was Touche Ross's argument for the appointment of senior staff in each police force with specific responsibility for the management of all forensic work undertaken within the force and for the commissioning of all forensic work undertaken by outside agencies. Initially designated as 'scientific support managers', these new post-holders (civilians in some forces, sworn officers in others) took financial and administrative charge of all relevant specialist services including crime scene examination, the force's laboratory, fingerprint and photographic departments and forensic submission units. All research on police uses of forensic science since the 1980s has been informed by an implicit or explicit recognition of the importance of the performance of this role for understanding the quality of the delivery of forensic support within UK policing in general and differences in the effectiveness of different police forces in particular.

A second set of recommendations by Touche Ross called attention to the role of crime scene examiners (then usually called 'Scenes of Crime Officers') in the forensic process. Research indicated a wide variation among forces in the staffing levels of examiners and corresponding variations in the proportions of criminal investigations (especially volume crime investigations) which were supported by their collection and interpretation of forensic evidence. Touche Ross presented these seemingly unplanned variations to argue for the need for Home Office direction in deciding the most effective staffing levels and in improving recruitment standards and training within this increasingly civilianised staff group. While the Home Office did provide direction ('staffing levels should allow an average annual maximum of 600 cases per SOCO to allow time for satisfactory examination of scenes' (Tilley and Ford 1996)), and recruitment and training standards were markedly improved, almost all subsequent research has continued to scrutinise the ways in which the work of this staff group necessarily shapes the essential initial stages of any investigation to which forensic science support may be relevant.

Many of the recommendations made by Touche Ross were subsequently endorsed and elaborated by the Audit Commission (1991) in their demand for the collection by individual forces of annual statistics 'on scene examination, fingerprints, forensic science and photography' and the analysis and reporting of these differences between forces by an unspecified 'central body'. But another report by the Audit Commission – on the quality of crime investigation in the early 1990s – provided an additional opportunity for all of those concerned to expand the uses of forensic science in support of police investigations in the UK. The importance of this report – and the 'intelligence-led' model of policing that it endorsed – is described in the next section of this chapter.

The rise of intelligence-led policing

The general introduction of new conceptions of crime management entered into aspects of police work at a time when increasing levels of public spending on policing were met by both rising crime and a decline of public confidence in the criminal justice system. Between 1981 and 1992 recorded crime in England and Wales had risen by over 70 per cent. In addition, clear-up rates had fallen from 41 per cent in 1979 to 27 per cent in 1992 (Audit Commission 1993). The response to this 'crisis' in policing was shaped both by the commitment to apply the principles of NPM already described, and also by the introduction of new conceptions and methods designed to improve the quality of criminal investigation practice. The Audit Commission, which characterised police investigations in 1993 as poorly organised and largely reactive, argued for the introduction of a 'proactive intelligence-led crime management approach' (1993: para 78). In this new approach, the police were increasingly expected to act 'proactively in relation to perceived risks, putting substantial effort and resources into planned strategies to identify and to "target" offenders, locations or activities that [appear] to present a sufficient level of threat or nuisance to the community to merit attention' (Maguire and John 1995: 68).

Since the early 1990s, 'intelligence-led policing' has become an essential feature of contemporary policing practice (see for example Gill 1998; John and McGuire 2003; Tilley 2003). The main elements of intelligence-led policing are:

- the targeting of known active offenders;
- the management of crime and disorder 'hotspots';
- the investigation of linkages between crimes and the emergence of crime series; and
- the application of partnership preventative measures.

The approach envisages that each of these elements will be supported by the provision of an evidence base of 'criminal intelligence', a term which is often defined rather loosely, but which generally refers to 'information that has been interpreted and analyzed in order to inform future actions of social control against an identified target' (Innes *et al.* 2005: 42). For Tilley (2003) the main organisational corollary of these developments has been the creation of specialist units within police forces to gather, evaluate, coordinate, analyse and disseminate such information.

The growth of such 'intelligence units' has required, and in turn encouraged, the development of new technological systems which facilitate the recording and interrogation of increasingly varied types of information held by the police and other state agencies. It is widely acknowledged that the effectiveness of this mode of policing is highly dependent on the existence of a comprehensive 'organisational memory' (see Marx 1988; Innes *et al.* 2005) containing various kinds of crime-relevant information, and whose construction, growth, maintenance and dissemination are all reliant on computer-based technologies of storage and communication. The development and deployment of intelligence in this way demands that the 'organisational memory' is developed to improve its knowledge about, and be more effective in intervening in, criminal activities: in particular, in knowing where, how, when, why and against whom to take action. The approach aims to capture certain individuals within an 'intelligence circuit': that is both a 'circuit of surveillance' designed to monitor and watch certain suspects (Williams and Johnson

2004) and a 'circuit of civility' in which their behaviour is assessed and measured (Gerlach 2004: 166). In short, an emphasis is placed on actively targeting certain individuals in order to intercede in their activities either to prevent their potential commission of criminal acts or, failing that, to quickly detain them following their offending.

Four years after the Audit Commission report of 1993, Her Majesty's Inspectorate of Constabulary published *Policing with Intelligence* (HMIC 1997) which outlined the key aspects needed to develop an 'integrated intelligence structure'. Like the Audit Commission, the report focused on the need to marry intelligence gathering with effective operational activities designed to reduce costs and raise detections. Particular attention was given to exploiting surveillance devices and CCTV as well as undercover investigations and the use of informants (Ratcliffe 2002). In addition to this a more general commitment to expanding the uses of science and technology to inform investigative actions has been pivotal to the operational implementation of intelligence-led policing. The National Intelligence Model (NIM), developed by the National Criminal Intelligence Service and adopted by ACPO in 2000, makes science and technology (or what it terms 'system products') central to successful intelligence-led investigations. The NIM, described in the National Policing Plan 2005–2008 as a 'cornerstone' of policing in England and Wales, provides a model of policing which attempts to ensure that all potentially useful information is fully researched and analysed to develop intelligence capable of providing strategic direction within police investigations. The need for implementing such a model was significantly heightened by the Bichard Inquiry's examination of police intelligence systems following the murder of two schoolgirls in Soham, Cambridgeshire. The Bichard Inquiry, set up to assess the effectiveness of intelligence-based record keeping and information sharing across state agencies, recommended significant improvements in intelligence collection and exchange. This was in light of the discovery that by the time the perpetrator had committed the offence, he had already been investigated by the police on at least ten previous occasions on suspicion of rape, underage sex, indecent assault and burglary. In particular the inquiry suggested the introduction of a national information technology system for the police intelligence system, the improvement of the Police National Computer, and a new code of practice on information management.

In many ways, the NIM provided an existing framework through which to achieve the recommendations made by Bichard. Its infrastructure is designed to harness the three levels of police work (at Basic Command Unit, Force, and National levels) in order to improve the flows of information and communication between them. However, the central strategy of the NIM is to gather intelligence to target individual offenders and 'potential offenders' and work to improve investigative efficiency in general, but also to achieve the objectives of increased detection and crime reduction in particular. At the centre of models like the NIM, and other strategies designed to improve intelligence-led policing, are conceptions about the types of individuals who should be targeted. These individuals may be previously convicted offenders, but they may also be previously known suspects who have no formal criminal record. It is this latter group which is central to the crime management strategy of identifying and intervening in the 'risky conduct' of individuals in order to both prevent and reduce crime.

Despite arguments by critics like Maguire and John (2005: 69) who assert that the underlying rationality of the NIM continues to co-exist with 'more traditional, reactive forms of crime investigation', intelligence-led policing remains foregrounded in contemporary government accounts of the promise of effective crime management. However, it is noticeable that early emphasis by the Audit Commission and others on the central importance of information collection and collation to the expansion of police intelligence capability paid little attention to the potential contribution of forensic information to any emerging model of intelligence-led policing. In part this may reflect the fact that the uses of forensic science in the late 1980s remained predominantly reactive, case-based and corroborative. Yet a series of changes in forensic practice that took place during the last decade of the twentieth century resonated closely with the central aims and general tactics of intelligence-led policing, and made possible the inclusion of forensic science information within an expanded understanding of intelligence-led policing in general. In particular, the establishment of electronically searchable fingerprint and DNA databases containing the trace biometrics of potentially recidivist offenders was easily characterised as offering powerful forensic intelligence for proactive use. In addition, the expanding collection and speculative searching of unidentified crime scene marks and stains supported by investment in information technology, supplemented the previous and more limited efforts to make links between a series of crimes carried out by a single or several suspects. Accordingly, in the remainder of this chapter we will focus on how these new uses of DNA, and physical evidence more generally, have become pivotal in the implementation of the political and operational frameworks described above.

Using physical evidence – research and evidence

Efforts to find ways of exploiting forensic science potential in order to achieve the aims and objectives of these new policy and policing frameworks can be traced to a joint agreement between the FSS and the Crime Committee of ACPO in Autumn 1991 to fund a research programme with the aim of 'making forensic evidence more effective and efficient' (Saulsbury *et al.* 1994: 1). The Police Foundation carried out the first study in this intended programme and its report introduced the key themes that have dominated all subsequent research in this area. These include: the lack of recognition given to the specialist knowledge and skills of crime scene examiners; low levels of police satisfaction with the turnaround times for services provided by forensic laboratories and information provided by those laboratories; and widespread concerns about the cost and affordability of forensic services following the introduction of direct charging regimes in the early 1990s.

In January 1994, a joint ACPO/FSS seminar was held at Bramshill Police Training College to discuss police uses of forensic science in support of criminal investigations and, specifically, the relationship between police forces and the FSS. Following the seminar, a steering group jointly chaired by the ACPO Lead on Forensic Science (D.G. Gunn of Cambridgeshire Police) and the Chief Executive of the FSS (Janet Thompson) commissioned and jointly resourced three projects: 'an environmental audit of forensic science provision'; a 'review of charging systems'; and 'guidelines for good practice in the use of forensic science'. Described by Thompson as part of 'an extensive programme of work aimed at improving the awareness, usefulness, scope and value of scientific support in the policing process' (Saulsbury *et al.* 1994: v), the resulting research provided an important assessment of the place of forensic science in criminal investigations in the mid-1990s. The most important project within this programme was carried out between July 1994 and September 1995. One report of this work was published as a 'diagnostic paper' in the Home Office 'Crime Detection and Prevention Series' (Tilley and Ford 1996), and another in the Home Office 'Police Research Series' (McCulloch 1996). In addition, a set of good practice guidelines developed by the project team – 'Using Forensic Science Effectively'

– was also produced and circulated to scientific support units in all forces in England and Wales. While neither of these papers mention the role of the Audit Commission, it is interesting that the authority of the Commission was used in support of the guideline document which credits all three agencies as its joint source (ACPO/FSS/Audit Commission 1996).

The two studies (by Tilley and Ford, and McCulloch) provided the most detailed and systematic examinations of the uses made of forensic information and expertise within the police service in the early 1990s. Yet the poor quality of police data available to their research imposed severe limitations on the conclusions they could offer concerning the effective uses of particular forensic technologies in general and DNA profiling in particular. Because of the timing of the work, neither the research report nor the good practice guidelines it contained provided detailed discussion of the emerging uses of the NDNAD (the fieldwork was largely carried out before the establishment of the NDNAD in 1995 and some years before state support for routine DNA analysis and databasing). Perhaps for this reason, Tilley and Ford's comments are understandably cautious:

There were initial fears among a number of SSMs and forensic scientists that the development of the DNA database might siphon funds from budgets allocated by forces for other forensic analysis. Early indications are that forces appear generally if not universally to have set aside a separate sum for DNA database work, although estimating needs is problematic since there are widely varying estimates of the proportion of scenes which will yield stains susceptible to DNA profiling. Any longer term effect of the DNA database will presumably depend in part on its outcome effectiveness which has obviously yet to be evaluated. (Tilley and Ford 1996: 42)

The multi-agency project, of which the research was only one element, used the essentially negative findings of the two studies to reinforce arguments about the necessity for wholesale improvements in current standards in the collection and utilisation of scientific information for intelligence and evidential purposes. These improvements were heavily promoted in 'Using Forensic Science Effectively' (ACPO/FSS/ Audit Commission 1996), a document that was widely disseminated among forces and which was heavily endorsed by senior staff in the FSS and ACPO. Insofar as it identified and commended examples of 'best practice', 'Using Forensic Science Effectively' also served as a promissory note to government, suggesting what could be achieved by those police forces who were fully competent in the deployment of a quickly expanding repertoire of forensic technologies. Interestingly, in the good practice guidelines, the critical stance of the Tilley and Ford report on the chronic shortcomings of 'performance indicators' as primary research data was used to support a demand for the 'urgent' development and use of performance indicators capable of measuring not only the 'internal efficiency' of scientific support units but also the 'success of scientific support units in supporting the investigative process' (ACPO/FSS/Audit Commission 1996: 40). In relation to the latter, the document suggested that any assessment of 'success' should be based 'not just on how much fingerprint and other forensic evidence was collected, but how much intelligence was supplied, evidence provided, and how many crimes were cleared as a result' (p. 13). Subsequent commentaries by HMIC, the Home Office and others on the use of forensic science by the police have all emphasised the content of the 'guidelines' document rather than the diagnostic papers when seeking to extend the influence of, what Thompson described as, a 'truly collaborative effort' and Gunn described as an exemplification of 'FSS/Police partnership in action'.

Establishing effective uses of the NDNAD

Given the underdeveloped state of research on the police uses of forensic sciences prior to 1994, the absence of a strong evidence base for the assessment of the value of DNA profiling to a wide range of criminal investigations before the establishment of the NDNAD is hardly surprising. Although at the time parallels were drawn to the longstanding use of fingerprint databases, limited research evidence showed that prior to 1995 the number of volume crime scenes from which DNA was collected was very small in comparison to the number of such scenes at which fingermarks were found, and that given this fact, the contribution of a DNA database of offenders to improving the detection of volume crime was necessarily a matter of future hope rather than existing experience.

Initial financial support for the establishment of the database and the development of DNA profiling was given to the FSS, but no equivalent funding was provided to police forces (apart from a sum of £3 million spent on 'raising awareness' of the value of DNA profiling and databasing across the police service). Instead, individual forces were charged for each sample profiled and each profile and sample stored by the FSS. Because of this funding regime (and concerns about rising expenditure on forensic science), at first most forces limited the sampling of suspects to those arrested for sexual and violent offences and some burglaries (especially of domestic dwellings) during the early years of the NDNAD. This meant that, while the database grew, its rate of growth was slow and, as a consequence, the matches derived from it were correspondingly fewer than had been hoped. Furthermore, delays in the expansion of FSS processing facilities meant that increased submissions occasioned substantial backlogs in profiles being loaded onto the database.

These problems – in part as a consequence of government demands for the speedy implementation of the database prior to much practical experience of what would be involved in collecting samples from crime scenes and criminal suspects, loading them onto a database and communicating results of matches to individual forces (as well as recording the results of all of these processes) – were reflected in what have been described by others as the 'critical findings' of two studies commissioned by the Home Office and completed a year after the establishment of the NDNAD (Burrows 1996 and Steventon 1996). Since neither has been published, their detailed results remain unavailable, but a later report does refer to the existence of operational difficulties with the early implementation of the database. However, despite the absence of a strong evidence base endorsing its effective uses across the 43 forces of England and Wales, the early days of the NDNAD were marked by a series of statements by the FSS, by ACPO, and by HMIC and the Home Office, which re-emphasised the general promise of DNA profiling and databasing as a new resource, with huge potential for increasing the effectiveness of criminal investigations including the investigation of volume crime.

Since the establishment of the NDNAD in 1995 the network of actors and agencies described in earlier chapters of this book has gradually constructed and applied two emergent approaches to the 'shaping of conduct into the optimisation of performance' (Dean 1999: 168) in police uses of forensic science in general and DNA in particular. The first approach has been to 'model' the forensic process in a way that facilitates an understanding of, and improvements in, its apparent capacity to contribute to crime detection; the second approach has been to impose on all 43 police forces an agreed series of measurements capable of representing and comparing differences in patterns of scientific support deployment of forensic DNA technology across England and Wales.

Soon after the NDNAD 'went live' the major stakeholders in its use began to make a series of claims about emerging changes in the use of DNA profiling in support of both routine and exceptional policing. For instance, the Chief Scientist of the FSS asserted in 1998 that 'there are now more stains analysed from undetected crime scenes than there are stains analysed within normal casework procedure' (Werrett and Sparkes 1988: 58). The distinction made here – between 'undetected crime scenes' and 'normal casework' – is an important one. Prior to the establishment of the NDNAD and a correlative change in the enthusiasm for the collection and analysis of biological material from crime scenes, a number of forces had submission policies for volume crime investigations in which such material would only be sent for analysis when suspects had already been identified:

> Traditionally forensic science has been part of a supply chain: samples would be obtained from scenes and suspects, some information with regard to the offence would be supplied to the laboratory. The laboratory would carry out examinations, a report would be produced that would go the Prosecution Service, or indeed the Defence, and finally where appropriate a court case would ensue. Through information being provided by the DNA Database the laboratory is now instigating investigations. Inceptive intelligence information produced by the National DNA Database is leading to new forms of crime investigation that are now becoming integrated within police procedures in the UK. (Werrett and Sparkes 1998: 58)

We have already noted in an earlier chapter that a series of important developments in laboratory technology between 1995 and 1998 made possible improvements in the analysis of crime scene DNA, which in turn contributed to an increase in the quantity and quality of forensic intelligence available to police forces. In addition to the FSS/ACPO pilot projects which disseminated knowledge of these improvements, the FSS also used available data on the collection and use of several types of forensic intelligence (especially, but not exclusively, fingermarks and DNA profiles) to construct a general 'crime reduction model' which became an important rhetorical resource in subsequent discussions of the funding and effectiveness of forensic DNA profiling in England and Wales. The model represented an idealised version of the potential contribution of increasingly routine crime scene DNA profiling and the NDNAD to crime detection and reduction. Described by their Director of Service Delivery as 'crude but powerful', one year's data on the examination of 'property crime' (including car crime, dwelling house burglaries and burglaries of non-dwellings) were used to represent 'attrition' in the investigative process, in other words the main stages in the filtering process which reduces the number of cases that go forward at each stage of the criminal justice process, between its beginning (with an offence being reported to the police) and its end (with the 'bringing to justice' of an offender through a variety of forms of disposal). In this FSS model only those stages that involved the collection, analysis and deployment of forensic science (especially fingerprinting and DNA profiling but also including toolmarks and shoemarks) were given detailed attention and assigned numerical value. In terms of genetic information, these were largely:

- the proportion of scenes of crime at which biological material suitable for DNA profiling may be found;
- the proportion of these samples from which DNA profiles may be constructed and matches made;
- the proportion of these matches that may contribute to the detection of the crime in question;
- the number of admissions of further offences that may be made by those charged with the crime; and
- by inference, an estimation of the further deterrent effect on those offenders.

While the model did not estimate the proportion of scenes of recorded crime which could be forensically examined, it suggested that DNA material was potentially discoverable from 5 per cent of those examined and that there would be a 30 per cent match rate when profiles derived from these examinations were loaded onto the NDNAD. Furthermore the model did not provide a figure for the 'conversion' of these matches into detections, but instead estimated a 'conversion rate' of 60 per cent for the four main types of forensic identification evidence (DNA, fingerprints, shoemarks and toolmarks) added together. It also suggested that each detection would secure the admission of a further two offences by the offender.

Despite the acknowledgement by the FSS of problems in the detailed figures, and the contestability of certain inferences drawn from them, the model was sufficiently plausible to support an argument to the government of the value of increasing the numbers of genetic profiles held on the NDNAD 'to a size similar to the fingerprint database'.

Furthermore, the capacity of the police and the FSS to accomplish the levels of detection (and eventually reduction) predicated by the model rested on improving the 'front and back ends of the supply chain' – in other words, on improving police operational performance in the collection of more suspect and crime scene samples at the beginning of the chain and in the effective use of intelligence derived from the analysis of resulting DNA matches and mismatches at the end of the chain.

These various claims and promises persuaded government ministers of the potential benefits of expanding the NDNAD, but there remained the difficult issue of how long it would take before its potential usefulness could be maximised. It is reported that the response of the then Home Secretary Jack Straw, to the suggestion that it would take 14 years for the NDNAD to reach the size of the fingerprint database on current growth forecasts, was to insist on a plan for this growth to be accomplished within a much shorter period, of four to five years at most. The provision and acceptance of this plan in the form of a particular government-funded 'programme' marked a dramatic improvement in the potential for the growth of the NDNAD and a corresponding rise in its usefulness for the investigation of crime.

The expansion programme

The DNA Expansion Programme, established in 1999, and originally designed to run until 2004, provided dedicated funding to individual police forces for 'the taking and processing and loading of CJ and SOC [scenes of crime] samples to the Database, the employment by the police of the necessary associated support personnel and equipment and the establishment of the DNA Liaison Panel meetings' (NDNAD Annual Report 2003).

The first stage of the Expansion Programme used a 'matching' method of funding that consisted of two elements. First, the Home Office allocated £17 million of the 2000/2001 programme budget to each police force (in proportion to their size); second, each force was required to match this figure from their own budget and also to spend all of these earmarked funds on the accumulation and processing of subject samples and crime scene submissions. The bulk of this expenditure by forces thus became income for the FSS and other forensic suppliers and facilitated further investment in laboratory facilities and staffing provision.

On 31 August 2000, just six months into the first year of the programme, the then Prime Minister Tony Blair announced the addition of £109 million (£25 million in 2001/2002; £42 million in 2002/2003; £42 million in 2003/2004) to the £34 million already committed for the first two years. It seems that these funds were not allocated for any fixed use, but a condition of the grant was that forces had to continue to spend £17 million nationally on DNA sampling for the years 2000/2001, 2001/2002 and 2002/2003. ACPO enquiries among forces suggested that increases in the number of SUBJECT and crime scene samples submitted for profiling and databasing necessitated additional expenditure on personnel to collect and process these samples, along with the resulting matches returned to forces by the NDNAD, and it was suggested that the additional grant money be spent on these staffing requirements. In view of this, the Home Office developed a distribution mechanism which required forces to bid for additional funds for these purposes from the global figure of £109 million.

However, funding became even more complex when, three weeks after the Prime Minister's announcement on 24 September 2000, the Home Secretary announced an additional £59 million funding under the programme 'specifically for enhancing forces' ability to attend crime scenes' for the collection of DNA evidence. This 'enhancement' meant the employment of 'assistant crime scene examiners' to be used largely for the examination of a limited range of volume (especially vehicle) crime. This was a clear endorsement by government of a recommendation by Blakey in *Under the Microscope* (HMIC 2000) which recognised the success of Northamptonshire police who were the first force to have introduced this cadre of staff some years earlier.

In official publications, after September 2000, the two streams of funding were added together and the sum of £168 million was usually referred to thereafter as 'Phase 2 of the Expansion Programme'. Forces began to make bids for funding from this programme from November 2000 onwards. We have already indicated that the DNA Expansion Programme was intended to have a dual focus on the 'front end' (offender sampling and crime scene stain collection) and 'back end' (using DNA matches to improve detection) of the forensic DNA process. Certainly for the first years of the programme, greater emphasis was given to 'front end' issues, with the aim of databasing the profiles of 'all known offenders' or 'the whole of the active criminal population' and identifying and collecting DNA from 'all viable crime scenes'. The main target set at the beginning of the Expansion Programme was the databasing of all 'active offenders' by March

2004. The initial numerical estimate for the identity category 'active offender' was given as three million, but it was acknowledged by the ACPO Lead on forensic science in October 2000 that the numerical target was to be reviewed throughout the lifetime of the programme (with the 'true target' for SUBJECT sample profiles being to ensure the DNA sampling of anyone convicted of committing a recordable offence who does not already have a profile on the NDNAD). This target has subsequently changed to reflect the extension of police powers to take samples from all of those arrested on suspicion of involvement in a recordable offence.

Arrangements for the evaluation of the Expansion Programme were in place from its beginning with the formation of an evaluation group chaired by the ACPO Lead on forensic science. This group studied the performance data returns made by all forces for each quarter of the first year of the Expansion Programme and also undertook a study of the 'systems and processes' for the collection and use of DNA samples and profiles in a sample of five forces. The unpublished report of the DNA Expansion Programme Evaluation Group showed that there were many areas of difficulty and uncertainty in the first year of the operation of this large and ambitious national programme. The report separately discussed the performance of forces in three 'key stages' of the process of DNA collection and use: crime scene attendance, 'offender sampling', and 'actions following notification of a match'. Much of the report was concerned with the shortcomings in the data returns provided by forces, but it also identified a series of general organisational issues impacting on the success of the programme. These included: the absence of clear guidelines on how the new money provided to forces should be best spent; overly ambitious expectations of the level of improvements in detections that could be delivered from DNA profiling of crime scene samples; and poor levels of integration of scenes of crime staff with other investigators.

Similar, if not more forthright, criticism of the responsiveness of some forces to the opportunities presented by the Expansion Programme were made by David Blakey in his important Thematic Inspection Report of scientific and technical support for policing (HMIC 2000). For the Chief Inspector of Constabulary, the funds granted under the programme 'illustrate[d] a significant measure of faith that the police service can deliver what is expected of it' (HMIC 2000: vi). He also asserted that it was 'vital' that the police service responded to this 'substantial commitment' by showing 'its full commitment to the recovery of DNA material wherever possible in order to detect crime and reduce offending'. However, it is clear throughout the report that Blakey was not confident that the aims of the Expansion Programme were being achieved and he drew particular attention to three issues:

- the failure of many forces to expand the category of offences in connection with which DNA samples were taken from individuals (not all had expanded their collection from the original focus on domestic burglaries, violence and sexual offences);

- the failure of many forces to remove profiles from the database of those charged with offences against whom action was discontinued or who had been acquitted in court (he estimated there to have been 50,000 such profiles held on the NDNAD at the time of his inspection); and

- the large variations between forces in the rate at which their crime scene examiners were submitting DNA samples from scenes (e.g. in burglary investigations, the rate varied from a high of 7 per cent to a low of 1 per cent).

The importance of Blakey's assertions of the urgent necessity for improvements in the ability of forces to collect DNA samples and monitor their uses of DNA profiles was recognised in the decision to undertake a further HMIC inspection within 18 months of his report. This 'revisit' inspection was explicitly undertaken to assess the response of the police service to the recommendations contained in *Under the Microscope*. While many of the forces studied had improved some aspects of their performance, Blakey's comments were less than enthusiastic: 'Things are improving but sometimes too slowly despite the large amounts of money invested' (HMIC 2002: vi).

What had exercised HMIC and other observers was not simply the question of whether or not the NDNAD was growing at the rate expected. In fact statistics provided in Chapter 1 of this book clearly show the overall growth in both subject and crime scene samples loaded onto the database since its inception. Of more concern was continued variation between forces in their willingness to take as many subject samples as they were legally entitled to do, as well as in their rates of DNA recovery from scenes of crime. Furthermore, there remained the question of how effectively forces were using the genetic intelligence provided by the database; put most simply, how successful they were at converting DNA profile matches into detections. Both of these issues – of collection and subsequent use – were the focus of a joint ACPO/FSS intervention into the use of forensic science in two forces in the north-west of England: the Pathfinder Project. This research project was expensive but more ambitious than any previous research on police uses of forensic science. Its final cost was £1,157,079, although most of the resources were used to fund and support the work of project managers and a team of forensic examiners supplied by the FSS. It was agreed in advance of the announcement of the DNA Expansion Programme and funded directly from the Home Office Crime Reduction Programme.

The main aim of Pathfinder was to 'assess the effectiveness of applying enhanced forensic techniques' (especially 'Low Copy Number' DNA, footwear marks and toolmarks) to the examination of property (burglary and car) crime scenes. However, this original aim was augmented by an assessment of the impact of the first phase of the DNA Expansion Programme in the two forces. The findings of the study are too complex to report in detail here, but its most significant contribution to understanding police uses of DNA profiling and databasing was its claim to provide a new model for maximising the impact of forensic science on crime detection. While the earlier FSS model had suggested that 'forensic activity' (largely the collection of physical evidence at crime scenes, the analysis of that material and its use by investigators) leads to the detection of 0.9 per cent of recorded crime, the model provided by the Pathfinder team suggested that approximately 3.3 per cent of recorded burglary and auto crime offences could be detected through the effective collection and use of fingerprints and DNA, and that this figure could reach 3.9 per cent if these technologies were enhanced by the use of more sensitive (but expensive) DNA technologies, as well as increases in footwear mark and toolmark collection.

The attrition figures for the collection and use of DNA in different stages of the investigative process provided by this new model were more optimistic than those included in the earlier FSS model. Using performance data collected in the course of the project it asserted that 6 per cent of property crime scenes attended should yield relevant biological material and that profiles should be obtained from 60 per cent of this material using conventional technologies. Furthermore, 73 per cent of such crime scene profiles when loaded onto the NDNAD should match individual profiles already held on the database (in other places in the model NDNAD scene-to-person matches are expressed as a proportion of DNA material recovered from crime scenes, thus providing a 'match rate' of 44 per cent). The figure provided by this model for the conversion of DNA matches to detections (depending on the assumptions made, this figure is given as either 73 per cent or 80 per cent) is also significantly higher than that of the earlier FSS model (of about 60 per cent).

Subsequent studies have provided a range of data concerning DNA recovery rates, but one the most authoritative of these (Green 2007: 345) provides the following picture of median force DNA recovery rates from volume crime scenes in the year 2004/2005. During this period, DNA samples were recovered and profiled from 8 per cent of domestic burglaries attended, 10 per cent of other burglaries, 20 per cent of stolen motor vehicles and 6 per cent of thefts from motor vehicles.[1] Match rates for these crime scene profiles varied from a low of 36 per cent in cases of domestic burglaries to a high of 47 per cent in cases of theft from motor vehicles. It is clear from these data that while recovery rates now exceed that assumed in the models described earlier, match rates remain lower than anticipated.

Between May 2001 and March 2006, 182,612 crime scene sample profiles have been matched with 165,099 separate individuals. However since not all crime scene sample profiles are full profiles, 20 per cent of these comparisons resulted in matches with more than one suspect sample profile, with 132,178 single suspect matches being made from the total. Puzzlingly, however, the rate at which immediate matches are made whenever a new crime scene sample profile is added to the NDNAD rose quickly in the early years of the NDNAD (from 37 per cent in 1999/2000 to 42 per cent in 2002/2003), but has risen much more slowly over the last few years despite the continuing increase in the number of retained subject sample profiles. This rate (for all crimes), currently standing at 52 per cent, might seem surprisingly low in light of the government claim that the NDNAD contains the profiles of 'all known active suspect offenders', unless the 'churn rate' of these offenders is higher than expected and/or many of the retained crime scene sample profiles do not originate from offenders but from innocent individuals (including victims) whose biological material was collected.

It is also notable that the rate at which immediate matches are made when new subject sample profiles are added (where matches will be to previously unidentified crime scene sample profiles) is less than 2 per cent, suggesting that (with some exceptions) the utility of the NDNAD for detecting historically unsolved volume crimes may be limited.[2] Whether this is because the biological material recovered may not have originated from the offender, or for some other reason, is difficult to establish. However, this uncertainty is much less likely to occur in cases of serious crime where the significance of the location and type of biological material left at a crime scene may more easily be determined.

Refocusing the Expansion Programme

As concern grew among forces that Expansion Programme funding would not continue after 2004, the Programme Management Board (and others) began to emphasise the necessity for the police service to focus more sharply on the 'back end' of the investigation process in order to improve both knowledge and force performance levels of the contribution of DNA-derived intelligence to crime detection (and crime reduction). However, this has proved difficult largely because of acknowledged shortcomings in the quality of existing data in this part of the forensic process. The NDNAD has no responsibility to provide information about the uses made of DNA profile matches once they have been reported to the police force from which the crime scene sample originated. These data are collected by forces themselves and collated by the Home Office in order to aid force comparisons and identify good practice. It is widely acknowledged that forces historically have differed in their ability to provide accurate data on these latter stages of the attrition process, but also that these differences have diminished in the recent past.[3] It is also asserted that there is significant variation between forces both in the proportion of DNA matches achieved and in their effectiveness at converting these matches into detections.

The most recent national summary of these data was provided in a report of the Home Office Forensic Science and Pathology Unit on the first five years of the Expansion Programme (Home Office 2006). The report included (on page 12) the following summary of seven years of data on DNA matches and 'DNA detections' (cases where

Table 6.1 Match and detection rates 1998/1999 to 2004/2005

Year	DNA matches	DNA detections	Proportion of matches, resulting in detections
1998/1999	21,238	6,151	29%
1999/2000	23,021	8,621	37%
2000/2001	30,894	14,785	48%
2001/2002	39,084	15,894	40%
2002/2003	49,913	21,082	42%
2003/2004	45,269	20,489	45%
2004/2005	40,269	19,973	49%

DNA crime scene sample profiles were loaded on the NDNAD and subsequently recorded as sanctioned detections).

The figures show large increases in both DNA matches and DNA detections between 1998/99 and 2004/2005 (with a dip in the number of matches but a rise in the proportion of matches leading to detections in 2004/2005). Further data provided in this report and reproduced below also indicate a positive effect on the overall detection rate when crime scene DNA is found and successfully matched with subject DNA on the NDNAD, an effect which is especially marked in certain types of volume crime.

Table 6.2 Detection rates 2004/2005

Crime type	Overall detection rate	Detection rate when crime scene DNA profiles are loaded on NDNAD
All recorded crime	26%	40%
Domestic burglary	16%	41%
Other burglary	11%	50%
Vehicle theft	15%	24%
Theft from vehicles	8%	63%
Criminal damage	14%	51%

These statistics on detections have to be interpreted with particular care. There are large differences in the ways in which forces record and return these data and therefore a variation in the quality of the data available for further analysis. Also, and despite appearances to the contrary, the majority of the published statistics on matches and detections have not been derived from the analysis of individual cases as they pass through the attrition process, but from aggregate data which represent the volume of cases at each stage. Until the recent work undertaken by Green and others on the Police Standards Unit/Lanner Group Scientific Work Improvement Model, only the Pathfinder project and one other Home Office study of forensic intelligence packages (Barrow 2005) had been able to follow through the forensic trajectories taken by individual cases. As reported by Green (2007), Barrow's study of 230 DNA match and fingerprint identification intelligence reports showed that 124 of these resulted in detections (but figures for fingerprint identifications and DNA matches are not given separately). In the absence of data derived from more studies of this kind it remains very difficult to assess the real impact of DNA profiling and databasing on crime detection rates. Many government statements have commended the power of the NDNAD at supporting the investigation of crime, and there can be no doubt that it has added significantly to police effectiveness, but exactly how much and in what ways still remain relatively unexplored. Summary data on detections of the kind found in the tables above – data which begin life as a single police officer's judgment of the significance of a DNA match to the outcome of the complex chain of actions that make up criminal investigations – need very careful examination before being accepted as an adequate representation of how DNA matches assist in detecting crime.[4]

While HMIC and other's within the police force share a concern to develop 'comprehensive qualitative outcome measures' for the analysis of the contribution to criminal investigations of forensic intelligence in general, and DNA intelligence in particular, the small number of empirical studies carried out on this topic have not usually examined the detail of the organisational arrangements that are involved in routine and exceptional efforts to collect these and other trace materials. Instead, the majority of the reports referred to in earlier sections of this chapter have simply identified an outline sequence of actions (e.g. as 'scene attended', 'contact trace material collected', 'DNA profile matched', 'fingerprint eliminated', 'crime detected through forensic match', etc.), measured the occurrence of these actions among different aggregates, and then inferred reasons for any observed differences.[5] However, making speculative inferences about how any, why one, or many, of these actions may have been carried out is not an adequate surrogate for detailed research on the situated uses of the wide repertoire of forensic knowledge, technology and other routine and exceptional organisational practices that are used in and through the course of criminal investigations. These crucial practices need to be topics of study in their own right if we are to ground firmly an understanding of forensic investigations as a routine set of activities accomplished by practitioners in the course of their ordinary work.[6] Statistical measures of the 'outputs' and 'outcomes' of such work need to be supplemented by studies of the 'concerted human reasoning, perception, conduct and communication' (Coulter 1989: 19) that make up the reality of criminal investigations and only when such studies are carried out are we likely to know exactly what the uses of DNA profiling and associated forensic technologies are contributing to the success of contemporary crime investigation practices.

Conclusion

The NDNAD can be understood as both an achievement and an object of government policy. Political enthusiasm for its establishment was occasioned by the orchestrated claims of two of the key agencies involved – the FSS and ACPO. While the early days of the NDNAD were inevitably characterised by modest achievements, the introduction of the DNA Expansion Programme marked not only a dramatic renewal of government commitment but also provided a major stimulus to existing efforts by the Home Office and ACPO to find ways of measuring and optimising the performance of forces in their use of forensic science in general and DNA profiling in particular. Writing of techniques of government, Rose and Miller have suggested that:

> The world of programmes is heterogeneous and rivalrous. Programmes complexify the real, so solutions for one programme tend to be the problems for another. Things, persons or events always appear to escape those bodies of knowledge that inform governmental programmes, refusing to respond according the programmatic logic that seeks to govern them. (1992: 190)

The creation and expansion of the NDNAD are exemplary instances of this general process. Elsewhere in the world its success has been highly celebrated and it certainly provides a model which deserves emulation. However, it has been reliably reported that there have been times in the last four years when the difference between ministerial expectations and the delivery of detections and reductions directly attributable to DNA intelligence prejudiced the funding of the Expansion Programme. It is difficult to know whether this difference should be attributed to what may turn out to be the over-optimistic forecasts of effectiveness contained in the two models of forensic investigation provided by the FSS and by the Pathfinder research team, to the varied capacity of different police forces to engage fully with the promise of the programme, or to the limits of what any particular identity technology and its associated archive can contribute to the contingencies of criminal investigations. There is a fundamental connection between the inclusiveness of identity archives (including DNA databases) and the operational uses of the information they provide, but understanding the nature of that connection requires an exploration of the variety of investigative practices that both structure, and are structured, by their availability. In the absence of that exploration, both valorisations and critiques of the effective uses of DNA profiling and databasing remain subject to chronic dispute.[7]

Notes

1 It should be remembered that these recovery rates relate to those recorded crimes attended by crime scene investigators. There is considerable variation among forces in their rates of attendance at volume crime scenes as well as differences according to the type of crime. Green (2007: 334) provides the following median force attendance rates: 88 per cent of domestic burglaries; 49 per cent of other burglaries; 49 per cent of motor vehicle thefts; and 25 per cent of thefts from motor vehicles.

2 In fact even where matches are made between newly loaded subject sample profiles and volume crime scene samples that were loaded some months or years earlier, limitations on investigative resources together with other evidential issues may make the continued investigation – and eventual detection – of such crimes unlikely.

3 Commenting on both fingerprint and DNA identifications, Blakey (HMIC 2002) asserted that: 'Many forces still have a great deal of difficulty in managing the process of turning identifications into detections and this is rooted in a paucity of quality performance'.

4 Hazel Blear's House of Commons answer of 1 March 2006 asserted that statistics are not collected on serious crime DNA detections because these detections are achieved 'through integrated criminal investigation and not by forensic science alone'. This assertion unintentionally undercuts current government claims for the credibility of any figure of 'DNA detections' achieved in cases of volume crime too. This must be so, since no detections of any kind are possible 'by forensic science alone' and all investigations involve the integration of forensic elements alongside other intelligence sources.

5 There is no reason for surprise at this failure. Strathern (2000) has cogently argued that such 'audit' approaches to these kinds of work processes only take into account the actions that they most want to affect while taking for granted (by both presupposing and re-asserting) adequate knowledge of the enabling social processes and surrounding social contexts.

6 In the course of a recent paper on 'crime intelligence analysis', Innes et al. (2005) have pointed to the usefulness of the approach of Lynch (2003) and Knorr-Cetina (1981) in providing analytical resources for such studies. We would add to these science and technology studies the recent work of Jasanoff and her colleagues (2004) which uses the concept of 'co-production' to emphasise the ways in which science and technology 'both embed and [are] embedded in social practices, identities, norms,

conventions, discourses, instruments and institutions – in short in all the building blocks of what we term the social' (Jasanoff 2004: 3).

7 Recent examples of contributions to this dispute include Staley and Wallace (2004), Webb *et al.* (2005), and McCartney (2006a, 2006b, 2006c).

Chapter 7

Governing the NDNAD

Granting that high standards are a sine qua non for the responsible use of DNA tests does not, of course, amount to saying that technical standards are the only issue of concern in relation to this infant technology. Indeed, in a speech to a symposium at Harvard University in the fall of 2000, Reno herself struck a deeper, more humanistic note, saying that the challenge is to learn how to govern, rather than be governed by, the power of DNA. If the problem is the broad one of governance, not simply the narrower one of standard-setting, what role should experts expect to play in that process? ... We need expert bodies like the [National] Commission [On the Future of DNA Evidence] to help us understand and mediate our relations with DNA-based techniques. In turn, the experts must learn to see their role as integral to democratic governance in what scientists have termed the age of genetics, and to conduct their affairs accordingly. (Jasanoff 2004: 342)

Introduction

In Chapter 5 we described the ways in which a series of legislative provisions has created the legal framework within which the police may legitimately employ DNA sampling and comparison in support of crime investigation. However, since the NDNAD rests on no single statutory instrument, it is necessary to look elsewhere in order to understand the arrangements which oversee its operation.

Of particular importance are the current arrangements for the custodianship of the NDNAD (which denote responsibility for the routine storage of genetic profiles, the comparison of profiles with one another, and the release of information about matches) and the governance of its use (how the accumulation, storage and use of genetic samples and profiles are managed and monitored).

This chapter explores the relationships that have developed between several public and private sector agencies involved in the custodianship and governance of the NDNAD. Of particular historic importance to this network has been the 'Memorandum of Understanding', between ACPO and the FSS, which provides an agreed framework with the aim of establishing and monitoring standards in forensic DNA analysis, controlling the uses that could be made of information derived from biological samples, and devolving significant operational responsibilities to the database Custodian. We also assess recent critical commentaries made in relation to the existing custodianship and governance arrangements of the NDNAD and discuss ongoing changes to these arrangements in the light of the transition of the FSS to a Government Owned Company (GovCo).

Governing the NDNAD: the 'Memorandum of Understanding'

A small network of institutional actors is directly involved in the operational uses of the NDNAD: the FSS (as the major supplier of profiles and until recently the database custodian); ACPO (with each of the 43 Chief Constables in England and Wales 'owning' the genetic samples, obtained from crime scenes and from individuals, and the information derived from them); the Home Office (as the government department providing policy steerage and dedicated financial support for the growing use of forensic science in support of crime investigation and now the NDNAD custodian); and a small number of private sector laboratories (authorised to analyse samples provided by police forces and submit the resulting profiles for loading onto the NDNAD).

These central roles of 'supplier', 'custodian', 'owner', and 'user', along with the rights and obligations that each implies, were initially established in a 'Memorandum of Understanding' (MOU) drawn up between two of the major agencies within this network – ACPO and the FSS – when the database was first established in 1995. While the origins of the MOU are obscure, and the framework has undergone minor revisions over the years of its existence, until recent changes described later in this chapter, it has been the primary instrument shaping NDNAD governance. When the custodianship of the NDNAD was transferred to the Home Office in 2005, the MOU was replaced with the 'ACPO Statement of Requirements' which covers essentially the same areas as the MOU.

The detailed organisational structures and operational responsibilities specified in the MOU are described as being determined by the application of a small set of underlying 'principles'. The most important of these are:

- the distinction between FSS ownership of the 'database' and individual police force ownership of both biological material (samples submitted for DNA analysis) and the profile data derived from them;

- the requirement for 'integrity in the management of the NDNAD in order to maintain public confidence in the use of DNA profiling'; and

- the characterisation of appropriate uses and users of the data (data are provided 'exclusively for the purposes of law enforcement', are 'available to authorised police users only for that purpose', can be used to provide 'intelligence and information to police forces', and 'will not provide evidence for use in court') (Forensic Science Service 2000).

While the FSS, as a corporate body, was often described as 'Custodian' of the NDNAD in the MOU, 'Custodianship' is also represented as a set of powers and duties embedded in a particular office occupied by a single individual – for most of its life, the Chief Scientist of the FSS. This key officeholder is in turn accountable to the body which is given overall authority for the management of the database by the MOU: the NDNAD Board (largely comprising FSS and ACPO representatives). This board is responsible for 'maintaining the integrity of the data held and the efficient and effective provision of NDNAD information and services' (Forensic Science Service 2000: 6) as well as monitoring the performance of the NDNAD using 'data and information on usage, input and outputs' provided by the Custodian (Forensic Science Service 2000: 11). The board itself has to 'direct the development of agreed data and criteria on which to assess current national performance and to evaluate development proposals' and is also expected to 'direct and sponsor management research and development with a view to identifying and promulgating good practice in the management of DNA by forces' (Forensic Science Service 2000: 11).

In the following sections of this chapter we will examine the ways in which the MOU, along with several other supporting documentary sources, has provided the framework in which the various participants involved with the operation of the NDNAD have recognised and responded to issues of governance and organisational accountability.

Contemporary 'principles' of governance

The organisation and regulation of the NDNAD are situated within patterns of governance prevalent in a range of contemporary social enterprises in general and public sector organisations in particular. England and Wales has no single model for the organisation of public sector services and it is recognised that there exists 'a diversity of organisations providing and delivering public services with constitutions, funding arrangements and operational procedures appropriate to the work they do' (Cm. 3557 1997: 7). This diversity reflects the character of the contemporary public sector as a network of public and private bodies operating within market or quasi-market social environments rather than as elements in a complex but unitary state bureaucracy. However, despite important differences between the various bodies within this network, a degree of uniformity in the ways that they are governed has been attempted through the application of a common discursive framework of 'public accountability' (see for example Cm. 3557, Cm. 3179 and Cm. 2850).

For the purpose of understanding the arrangements for the custodianship and governance of the NDNAD it is useful to discern three types of public accountability which have been pivotal to the formation and ongoing use of this technology:

- 'juridico-scientific accountability' is the requirement that organisational structures and operational procedures have sufficient integrity to satisfy legal requirements and resist adversarial – including scientific – challenge;

- 'administrative accountability' requires that economy, efficiency and effectiveness can be authoritatively established and assessed through various forms of audit appraisals; and

- 'civic accountability' requires that structures and processes are open, transparent and responsive to the wider civil society within which they operate.

In the remainder of this chapter we will discuss how these types of public accountability have framed the development and operational activities of the NDNAD.

Juridico-scientific accountability

Insofar as the law allows the NDNAD to be used to store and speculatively search DNA profiles taken from individuals and from crime scenes, the MOU recognises a responsibility on the part of the Custodian to establish and maintain 'appropriate protocols procedures and standards of performance required to ensure the reliability, compatibility and legality' (Forensic Science Service 2000) of all the data held on the database. Juridico-scientific accountability is universally recognised to be central to the establishment and uses of the NDNAD. Effective control over the management and uses of the database is seen by ACPO as largely subject to a legal framework which both enables and constrains how these data are managed as well as the uses to which they may legitimately be put. From such a perspective, both the system of database governance and the scope of allowable uses of DNA for operational purposes are the product of the legislative arm of government to which the police are ultimately responsible. A series of statutory instruments and government circulars is seen to provide the essential limits of legitimate action (for example, Home Office Circular 25/2001, updating HOC16/95). A wide range of organisational issues is involved in the exercise of these responsibilities, the most important of which are described below.

Standard setting

There are a number of ways in which the Custodian exercises a responsibility for setting standards for the operation of the database to 'ensure the reliability, compatibility and legality' (Forensic Science Service 2000) of all data held on it. First, the Custodian advises the Board on the DNA data that are to be used for the construction of profiles to be held on the database, along with the minimum standards that have to be met for each separate profile to be loaded and searched. Second, the Custodian has a duty to establish 'appropriate protocols, procedures and standards of performance' (Forensic Science Service 2000) for database entries, information derived from them, and for the reports provided to relevant users. Third, the Custodian sets standards for the specification of all collection kits that may be used by forces to take samples from individual suspects or volunteers and from scenes of crime. Finally, the Custodian advises the board on the suitability of laboratories wishing to become suppliers of data to the NDNAD.

In this latter instance, standards are set by reference to an external body, the United Kingdom Accreditation Service (UKAS), which assesses and, where appropriate, accredits laboratories seeking to supply profiles to the database. The ISO/IEC 17025 standards ('General Requirements for the Competence of Testing and Calibration Laboratories' and 'Supplementary Requirements for Accreditation in the Field of Forensic Science') along with the additional requirements stipulated by the Custodian are set out in the FSS document 'The National DNA Database Standards of Performance'. In summary:

All suppliers are required to use a documented protocol for DNA profiling which is acceptable to the Custodian. Suppliers must satisfy the Custodian that they are competent and licensed to use the technique, must adopt internal handling processes and procedures that conform to the rules of evidence, must carry out an internal quality assurance programme to the specification set by the Custodian and endorsed by the Home Office and must be UKAS accredited for their profiling services. (UKAS 2001: para 2.4)

The nature of the overall assessment by UKAS is specified by reference to further UKAS documents and international standards (including NIS46, NIS96, ISO25, ISO9000 and ASO9001).

Laboratory quality assessment and assurance

In addition to setting the scientific and procedural standards to be maintained by suppliers of information to the database, the Custodian is also responsible for monitoring the performance of suppliers against those standards. The Quality Assurance Programme includes the assessment of both 'declared samples' (where samples are submitted to the laboratory for criminal trials) and 'undeclared samples' (where samples are submitted by individual police forces as originating from criminal suspects). All instances of profiles supplied that are 'subsequently found to be in error' (Forensic Science Service 2000) are recorded by the Custodian, who also facilitates the checking of all near miss matches (matches on all but one allele). Successful completion of proficiency tests by all the staff involved in DNA analysis in each supplier laboratory is a condition of continued accreditation.

Data handling, data protection and database security

The MOU outlines the duty of the Custodian to establish and maintain arrangements for the safe and accurate transfer of data between profile suppliers and the NDNAD, as well as overseeing the accuracy, storage, management and deletion of profiles and the demographic data associated with them. Since March 2000, the Information Commissioner has been responsible for enforcing the provisions of the Data Protection Act (DPA) (1998) and ensuring that 'data controllers' (those who decide how and why 'personal data' are processed within their organisation) comply with its provisions. According to the DPA, 'personal data' include facts and opinions about an individual, as well as information regarding the intentions of the data controller towards the individual. The Secretary of State and ACPO are designated as data controllers of the NDNAD, and the Custodian as 'data handler' is required to ensure that access to, and use of, all records on the NDNAD and the PED are compliant with the Act. This includes the requirement to provide individuals whose information is contained on the NDNAD with details of any records that are covered by that legislation. The Custodian is also expected to provide a secure environment for the database and to make 'disaster recovery plans' to deal with serious failures in IT, accommodation or personnel. Access control to information on the NDNAD is limited by password protection and security is 'layered to meet the requirements of data protection legislation' (Forensic Science Service 2000: 9).

In some legal jurisdictions (e.g. Australia), the anonymity of profiles on the database is guaranteed by restricting information that would identify the source of the reference sample to the police force that supplied it. The arrangement in England and Wales is more complex. All persons arrested or summonsed are given a unique Arrest Summons Reference Number and barcode when police create a new record on the Police National Computer (PNC). Alongside the PNC record is an electronic CJ record on which is entered the same Arrest Summons Reference Number and barcode data along with the individual's name, date of birth, ethnic appearance code, gender code, police force in which the sample was taken, supplier laboratory, the type of DNA test and a numerical representation of the sample profile. The whole of the electronic record is transferred to the NDNAD by the police force which created it and the relevant information is also provided to the supplier laboratory which completes further information regarding the DNA analysis. Each PNC record should also be continually updated to show the developing status of any DNA sample taken from the individual and be marked with the appropriate description: 'Taken'; 'Held in Force'; 'Missing'; 'Destroyed'; 'Profiled'; 'Confirmed'; 'Rejected – Resampling is Permitted'; and 'Rejected – Resampling is not Permitted'.

These informational arrangements have largely been established in order to ensure that all individuals who are eligible for sampling are contained on the NDNAD and that such individuals are not sampled more than once (although the first Annual Report of the NDNAD stated that there still remains a large number of replicate profiles on the database). Since 2001 there has been a computer interface between the PNC and the NDNAD to ensure that high standards of record keeping are maintained. However, there are some older records on the NDNAD for which there are no PNC records. There is no link between the PNC and the arrest records of Scottish police forces who export profiles for inclusion on the NDNAD, and there is no link between the PNC and samples and profiles given voluntarily since these individuals cannot be given a record on the PNC. These arrangements for data management mean that identifying details about individuals are held on the NDNAD. The confidentiality of these details must therefore be secured by controlling access to information within the FSS itself and not simply in individual police forces.

Administrative accountability

The issues of judicial and scientific accountability described in the previous section are largely focused on the establishment, preservation and enhancement of the overall reliability of the NDNAD as an aid to criminal investigations in general. The efficiency of its routine operation and the effectiveness of its uses by individual police forces raise different questions. Although these questions have been a topic of discussion in the previous chapter, it is also important to note here that they have always played a central role in establishing and monitoring the framework and processes of NDNAD governance.

Procedure

Several sections of the MOU specify particular aspects of the relationship between the Custodian and its service users. For instance, the Custodian is expected to meet service level targets agreed with the board, provide the outline of a charging regime (costs recovered through charges for specific services at a level agreed with the board and reviewed annually), and provide a 'help desk to deal with enquiries from the police and other suppliers about specific DNA profiles submitted to the NDNAD and other matters associated with Custodianship' (Forensic Science Service 2000: 9). By far the most important aspect of the Custodian's procedural responsibility is that the loading, searching and matching of profiles on the NDNAD are carried out as speedily as possible so that information about matches reaches the police in a timely way. The MOU provides for speculative searches of newly loaded profiles against existing profiles to be made on a daily basis in order that any match identified is relayed to the supplier of the profile. Reports of matches are then issued as soon as possible to the forces who supplied the profiles (crime scene and/or CJ samples). In addition, the MOU requires the Custodian to make provision for the 'one-off speculative searching' of scenes of crime samples that have provided insufficient allelic data to be permanently added to the NDNAD. Despite not being loaded, such profiles can be re-checked against databased profiles 'at agreed specified intervals' (Forensic Science Service 2000).

Performance

We have already discussed the ways in which the measurement of the effectiveness and efficiency of NDNAD performance has been modelled on widespread efforts by several government bodies to audit the delivery of forensic science and its usefulness to policing. The late 1980s and early 1990s witnessed a series of positive evaluations of the potential of forensic science to contribute to the effectiveness of criminal investigations and prosecutions. In particular, both the House of Commons Home Affairs Committee (1988–1989) and the House of Lords Select Committee on Science and Technology (1992–1993) made strong arguments for the extension of existing budgetary provision for forensic science in support of crime investigation. These arguments rested on claims of cost-effectiveness, especially when compared with the costs of other investigative strategies, but neither Touche Ross (1987) nor the House of Lords Select Committee were precise about the possible level of efficiency gains or the general framework for measuring the contribution of forensic science to crime investigation and prosecution.

Civic accountability

We noted earlier that agreement on the form and content of the MOU, the major instrument governing the NDNAD, was achieved between participants in a small network of actors and agencies. For most of the policy makers, managers and users involved in that network, juridico-scientific and administrative forms of accountability have been of primary importance. In particular, they have focused on issues of 'evidential rigour', 'standard setting and quality assurance' and 'efficiency, effectiveness and cost-effectiveness' as the central preoccupations of governance. While issues of civic accountability have not been ignored, they have occupied a marginal role in structuring and informing the organisation and uses of the database.

Nevertheless, ACPO have long since recognised that the collection and retention of DNA profiles and samples raise some important issues regarding civic accountability that have not previously been raised by their ownership of other forms of personal information:

> Police fully recognise the sensitivity of maintaining DNA data on individuals on the National DNA Database and we accept the need for high standards of probity/integrity at all stages of the process. That includes the need for DNA profiles to be removed from the Database whenever a person is acquitted in a case for which a DNA suspect sample has been taken or that case is discontinued for whatever reason. Police also acknowledge the concern that people have about genetic information held on the National DNA Database being misused for purposes other than those for which it is originally gathered and stored. (ACPO Memo to House of Lords Select Committee on Science and Technology 2000 HL 115)

However, this memorandum identifies no particular measures designed to address the acknowledged 'concern' and further documentary elaboration of issues of public concern – and hence civic accountability – is foreclosed by the rhetorical claim that all 'social, ethical, legal and economic implications of the National DNA Database should be viewed in the light of its enormous success in helping to prevent and detect crime'.

Elsewhere in the world, various bodies largely independent of operational policing and criminal justice administration have been set up to consider the more general social and ethical implications of the growth of forensic DNA profiling and databasing (as well as the claims made for their efficacy in support of criminal investigations). These bodies have sometimes been formed as commissions who have worked in advance of the establishment of national or sub-national forensic DNA databases (most recently, in the Republic of Ireland) and sometimes to provide oversight of their subsequent development and uses. When the 1993 Royal Commission recommended the establishment of the NDNAD, although it provided no detailed discussion of its governance, it suggested the usefulness of an independent body with the remit to oversee forensic science. In addition, there have been several subsequent calls for the establishment of a body to exercise oversight of the NDNAD in particular. Most recently these have come from two significant public bodies. The House of Lords Select Committee on Science and Technology (2001: para 7.66) recommended that 'the Government should establish an independent body, including lay membership, to oversee the workings of the National DNA Database, to put beyond doubt that individuals' data are being properly used and protected'. The Human Genetics Commission (2002: 153) made several alternative suggestions of ways to make possible independent participation in the current arrangements for governing the NDNAD and to increase the transparency of its operation: 'at the very least, the Home Office and ACPO should establish an independent body, which would include lay membership, to have oversight over the work of the National DNA Database custodian and the profile suppliers'.

Until very recently, a reluctance to respond to such observations has meant that concerns identified as central to the civic accountability of forensic DNA profiling and databasing have not been fully addressed within the closed circle of NDNAD policy makers, managers and users. This set of concerns includes both general issues of independent scrutiny of the operation and uses of any such database, the appropriate degree of openness and transparency of its working, as well as more specific issues concerning the retention and permissible analysis of the original biological material and the extracted DNA from which database profiles have been constructed.

However, in July 2002, the Home Office announced that there would be a quinqennial review of the FSS. Although the original terms of reference for that review included no specific reference to the governance of the NDNAD, Robert McFarland, as leader of the review, was subsequently asked to consider the role of the NDNAD Custodian in light of the House of Lords and Human Genetics Commission's observations mentioned above.

The final report recommended major changes to the status of the FSS, which in summary amounted to changing its status from an Executive Agency of the Home Office with Trading Fund to a Private Public Partnership (with a short interim period of between 12 and 18 months as a Government Owned Company). McFarland also argued that as a corollary of these changes:

> the present custodian arrangements needed to be made more independent, more transparent and more accountable. The Review also acknowledges the concern over the fact that the Custodian role is not fully separate from that of the main supplier of DNA profiles to the database. Equally the Review accepts that there is an overriding public interest in maintaining the effectiveness and operational efficiency of the NDNAD. The Review is recommending that the NDNAD Custodianship is removed from the FSS. It is proposing that the NDNAD database becomes the responsibility of the NDNAD Board reconstituted into a (public sector classified) Company Limited by Guarantee (CLG), with an independent chairman but with a majority of the membership nominated by ACPO. (Home Office 2003: 3)

In the following sections of this chapter we discuss several of the main features of governance that arise from these recommendations and consider the extent to which they meet the kinds of concerns expressed by McFarland and a number of other recent commentators.

Oversight

There currently exists no independent oversight or controlling body which is able to scrutinise either the management of the NDNAD, the formal roles organised and specified by the MOU, or the routine practices of the Custodian, analysts and 'owners' of genetic samples which are supplied, processed and used in relation to the NDNAD. This absence of independent scrutiny contrasts markedly with the governance arrangements for medical DNA databases in England and Wales. It is also significantly different from the arrangements for the oversight of forensic DNA databases found in some other legal jurisdictions. In such contexts it is generally agreed that oversight bodies are chaired by a respected public figure and that a board will include a substantial representation of individuals who are unconnected with database custodianship or use, but at least some of whom have professional knowledge of relevant scientific and criminal justice matters.

Openness and transparency

It is often asserted that the maintenance of public confidence, or trust, in the operation of forensic as well as medical databases is partly dependent on the openness and transparency of their operation. It is important for civil accountability that individuals or relevant agencies have sufficient knowledge about their detailed workings to arrive at authoritative judgments of claims made, for example, concerning the confidentiality of records, the security of the database, performance levels, and the results of various quality assurance trials. Yet it is only recently that the first publicly available document has been circulated addressing these issues in relation to the NDNAD (the first National DNA Database Annual Report was issued in 2003).

Research

Since the first introduction of DNA profiling into criminal investigations there have been constant research-based innovations in technologies affecting the construction and interpretation of tissue samples and their storage and interrogation within databases. The FSS is very often described as a world-leader in these matters, although the research and development capacity of an increasingly market-driven organisation has often been described as problematic 'in the absence of long-term investment, direction and support from Government' (Roberts 1996: 43). While the MOU authorises the use of the NDNAD for 'specified research purposes to assist with law enforcement' (Forensic Science Service 2000: 7), it is unclear what range of 'specified research purposes' may be allowable, what is included as 'use of the NDNAD' and what independent mechanism exists for the assessment and approval (including the ethical dimensions) of any proposed projects.

All samples are held in the laboratories in which the profiling was carried out. The individual police force that supplied the relevant biological material (as crime scene stains or CJ samples) assert property rights over this material and pays an annual fee for its continued storage. Crime scene samples should be retained until the completion of a sentence served by the person convicted of the offence in relation to which the material was collected. In the case of CJ samples, retention will be indefinite. Important questions arise from the absence of formal arrangements governing detailed matters of ownership, use and long-term storage of these samples. Not least is the lack of an agency able to provide independent adjudication between the owners of the genetic samples and the individuals from whom they were originally taken (although any dispute over ownership could be subject to civil justice proceedings where genetic samples would be recognised as legitimate property).

Data-sharing

Genetic data used to represent individuality on the NDNAD are currently understood to have no additional diagnostic potential of interest to insurers, employers or medical practitioners. It is perhaps for this reason that NDNAD records are not characterised by the Information Commissioner as 'sensitive personal data'. However, the definition which the Information Commissioner uses to characterise sensitive personal data could include NDNAD profiles. For example, the Information Commissioner states that any information regarding 'racial or ethnic origin' should be deemed sensitive and personal. NDNAD profiles are now used to infer ethnic origin and the use of technologies to make such inferences is likely to increase in the future (we deal with this issue fully in Chapter 7). The Custodian of the NDNAD is subject to the 'principles of good information handling' as promulgated by the Information Commissioner, which state that data must be:

- fairly and lawfully processed;
- processed for limited purposes;
- adequate, relevant and not excessive;
- accurate;
- not kept longer than is necessary;
- processed in line with the data subject's rights;
- secure; and
- transferred only to those countries who ensure 'adequate protection for the rights and freedoms of data subjects' (the EEA, made up of the Member States of the EU, Norway, Iceland and Liechtenstein, is already recognised as affording such protection).

However, recent developments in trans-jurisdictional genetic data-sharing raise additional issues to those of 'adequate protection for the rights and freedoms of data subjects'. Insofar as different jurisdictions have a variety of laws concerning the sampling, profiling and retention of DNA from different categories of individuals, some care will need to be exercised in the design and execution of any automated system of data-sharing (and in the legislation which authorises its use). Arrangements will have to be made which recognise each jurisdiction's legislative provisions and agreements will have to be made about which categories of reference samples may be searched for matches (e.g. 'convicted offenders', 'unconvicted suspects', 'voluntary samples', etc.). In the meantime, and in the absence of such arrangements, it seems likely that necessary trans-jurisdictional data-sharing will take place either on a case-by-case basis by means of one-off speculative searches, or by the establishment of a dedicated international DNA database to which jurisdictions can add profiles that they believe to be relevant for international comparison (we address the future development of this practice in Chapter 8).

Conclusion

At the time of writing, a new governance model for the NDNAD is beginning to emerge, although it is not wholly clear which individuals and groups are involved in determining its details. The NDNAD Annual Report 2005–2006 describes some of the recent changes, including the establishment of a NDNAD Strategy Board, chaired by the ACPO Lead on forensic science and with a membership comprised of APA, Home Office, ACPO and ACPOS representatives along with two Human Genetics Commission members (one of who is described as the 'principal advisor to the Board on ethical matters'). Plans are also in hand for the establishment of an independent Ethics Group to be 'drawn from a wider audience'. However since the report also states that 'The Board has discretion over whether or not to act on any advice provided on ethical matters' by the current individual or the future group, it is not obvious what powers the Ethics Group will have. In addition, a new 'Forensic Science Regulator' will be expected to play an important role in the oversight of a range of forensic science matters, but that role too has yet to be fully specified.

In a range of public statements and reports government ministers and Chairs of the NDNAD Board have consistently declared a commitment to openness, transparency and accountability in the operation of the NDNAD, including its use for research. They have also recognised the importance of these values to the maintenance of public confidence in police use of forensic genetics. The degree to which discussions of changes in its governance structure themselves remain open, transparent, accountable and inclusive provides an interesting test of the depth of these commitments, and in this respect their record has been rather mixed. For example, the current government has never issued the McFarland report as a fully public document (although a copy was deposited in the House of Commons library), and promises to publish NDNAD Board minutes on the Home Office website have yet to materialise.

In 2008 the contract granted to the FSS to operate the NDNAD will end and the database will be open to tender from private forensic companies. With so many current governance arrangements still 'under consideration' it is vital that these new arrangements are solidified quickly to oversee this vast collection of samples and profiles. The new 'Regulator' role (along with the establishment of a 'Forensic Science Advisory Council' which seemingly will 'advise' the Regulator) may prove crucial in providing much needed public accountability for the uses made of this genetic collection when it potentially leaves the operational administration of the FSS and is managed within the private sector. Yet specification of the Regulator's powers and duties and the relationship between the Regulator and other agencies, including the question of to whom the Regulator will be accountable, remains vague at the time of writing.

Chapter 8

Current developments and emerging trends

Introduction

As we have argued in previous chapters, a combination of scientific and technological innovations, alongside a comprehensive programme of legislative reform and fiscal investment, has meant that the uses of the NDNAD have expanded dramatically and quickly. The growing size of the database, its promotion as an essential tool for crime control, and its status as an exemplar of 'intelligence-led policing', have together prompted a range of commentaries about its current operation and speculations about its future development. Most of these interrogations focus on two key areas: first, the trajectory of the inclusion regime of the NDNAD and the possibility that it may expand further; and second, the emerging innovations in both profiling and databasing technologies and their imagined uses in future criminal investigations and prosecutions. Often these issues are brought together in contemporary debates, such as those which focus on the possible creation of a universal forensic database, the connectivity between this and other genetic databases, as well as those which consider the additional uses which could be made of DNA samples and profiles by police investigators and other state and commercial agencies. In this chapter we address and explore these debates and focus on the various possible futures that may exist for the NDNAD. We provide a commentary on what the likely developments in profiling and databasing may be and which of these potential changes are most desirable to what groups.

Database futures: changing the inclusion regime

The most enthusiastic proponent of the collection and storage of DNA profiles by the police might conclude that, following an ambitious programme of fiscal investment and legislative innovation, the effective maximisation of the NDNAD 'population' in England and Wales has been achieved. Given its legislative provision, England and Wales can now claim to have the greatest scope for retaining and continually searching samples taken from all criminal suspects. Because such provisions empower the police to collect samples without consent from a wide group of individuals (including newly suspected individuals along with those already convicted), it may appear that the legal limits of sampling have now been reached. In other words, it is often assumed that the database is now 'complete' save for the addition of new individuals – suspects or volunteers – who are added year on year. The idea of the NDNAD being 'complete' is embedded in the Home Office target to capture the 'active criminal population' on the database which, calculated at its current size, has been achieved. As the Home Office now state on their website, 'the majority of the known active criminal population is now registered' on the database, even if this category includes 'active suspect offenders' along with those who have been subject to judicial disposal.

However, since the database went live in 1995 the addition of new categories of persons has been central to its development: from the inclusion of profiles taken from the convicted since 1995, to those charged since 2001, to those arrested since 2003, along with profiles from volunteers, those convicted before 1995 and still in custody, and those held under the Mental Health Act. This gradual expansion of the categories of individuals sampled, profiled and databased suggests that (for some stakeholders at least), there remains further scope to make the database even more inclusive. For this reason, it is worth considering how the database may develop in the future to include new categories of persons.

'Suspects' prior to arrest

One important category of persons who may be subject to compulsory sampling and databasing in the future is those who are subject to police attention prior to formal arrest. It may be difficult to imagine the police being empowered to take and database a compulsory non-intimate sample from persons before they are arrested, because such a provision would be antithetical to existing legal principles of individual bodily integrity. However, recent developments in police procedure make such a change highly possible. The Serious Organised Crime and Police Act 2005, made a significant amendment to the rules governing the taking of fingerprints without consent. The amendment, contrary to all prior understandings and legal arrangements for the taking of fingerprints, allows the police to compel individuals to provide fingerprints *prior* to arrest in particular circumstances – such as during questioning about traffic or other offences – where 'the name of the person is unknown to, and cannot be readily ascertained' by a constable or there is 'reasonable grounds for doubting whether a name furnished by the person as his name is his real name'. The rationale for such a provision is that the police are enabled quickly to establish the identity of a 'suspect' when definite knowledge of personal identity is absent or there are sufficient grounds for suspecting that a personal identity given by the individual to the police is false.

As we argued in Chapter 2, these new provisions for immediate fingerprinting have been facilitated by the development and introduction of portable and handheld equipment to enable police officers to take digital finger scans which can then be instantaneously transmitted for comparison to records held on the National Automated Fingerprint Identification System. It is therefore important to recognise how this technological development has made possible a reshaping of the legal arrangements which govern the relationship between the police and citizens who come to their attention. In such cases, individuals cannot be easily categorised as 'suspects' since they have not been subject to formal arrest on suspicion of involvement in any crime, yet they may still be compelled to provide fingerprints. Therefore, while the ability to deploy such technology in certain circumstances may aid the work of the police, offering them a 'convenient' way to ascertain or disambiguate identity, the development, adoption and integration of a new technique have provided a warrant for changing the legislative arrangements for who may be compelled to submit their body to examination.

The existing provisions of the Serious Organised Crime and Police Act 2005 do not cover the taking of non-intimate samples and therefore do not empower the police to gather biological material suitable for DNA profiling. A current absence of technology that would allow the immediate DNA profiling of individuals through the use of portable devices, along with the infrastructure to make comparison of such profiles with existing collections of samples, might seem to

145

make the addition of DNA sampling to this supplemented regime of identification unlikely. Nevertheless, and even without the addition of DNA profiling, the new regime does constitute a major change in the relationship between the right of the individual to maintain bodily integrity and the powers of the police to interfere with it, at least as far as requiring digital fingerprints to be temporarily surrendered (if a declared identity is validated through such a check the digital record shoud be destroyed). In addition, it is worth noting that the traditional way in which fingerprints and samples have usually been bound together in legislation may provide an easily justified route for the future extension of the Act to include non-intimate samples once DNA profiling technology permits.

Offence categorisation

There is another, perhaps more immediate, way in which the inclusion regime of the NDNAD may be widened to database more individuals. This is through a redefinition of the types of offences, currently deemed 'recordable', which attract compulsory sampling. What makes an offence 'recordable', as opposed to an offence which is not, is that the offence is included in the National Police Records (Recordable Offences) Regulations. Currently included in the regulations are all offences which carry the possibility of a term of imprisonment and certain other non-imprisonable offences. The non-imprisonable offences which are included are subject to frequent revision and change over time. For instance, a range of new non-imprisonable offences has recently become subject to inclusion under the regulations and, as a result, became newly classified as 'recordable'. An amendment to the Regulations in 1997 introduced 42 new offences as recordable, a further five were added in 2000, and in 2003 the non-imprisonable offences of 'begging', 'persistent begging' and 'touting for hire car services' (taxi-touting) were included. There is tangible scope to extend further the definition of recordable offence to include more non-imprisonable offences in the future. If, as we have argued elsewhere (Williams and Johnson 2004a), the NDNAD is thought of as one instance within a much broader repertoire of instruments aimed at managing the 'risky conduct' of individuals, it is interesting to monitor how certain forms of conduct become subject to new forms of appraisal (such as begging) and how, as a result, certain individuals are easily moved into the 'suspect population'.

Currently, the government has begun a consultation on reforming PACE to allow the collection of fingerprints and DNA samples from all those suspected of a non-recordable offence. The government argues that:

> The current thresholds for taking and using fingerprints etc. create a number of inconsistencies. For example, fingerprints, samples and footwear impressions of a person arrested, reported, charged, summonsed or convicted for a non-recordable offence cannot be taken without consent to confirm or disprove their involvement in that offence or to create a record in a national searchable database that they have been arrested, reported, charged, summonsed or convicted.[1]

The use of the word 'inconsistencies' with respect to the powers afforded to the police by PACE is misleading. The existing distinction which PACE draws between recordable and non-recordable offences in relation to samples and fingerprints represents the outcome of considered and sustained deliberation on this matter by parliament. Parliament has repeatedly maintained this distinction in statute to mark an appropriate threshold at which the police are able to breach the bodily integrity of criminal suspects to obtain non-intimate samples without consent. Such a threshold is established in relation to an assessment of the degree of seriousness of an offence and its impact upon victims. That is why, for instance, the criminal offence of 'exceeding the speed limit' is not a recordable offence, but 'dangerous driving' is a recordable offence. The distinction is based on the degree of seriousness of each offence in terms of its impact on individual victims and society as a whole, its requirements in terms of policing and law enforcement, and the penalties that it should attract upon conviction.

Retention in Scotland and Northern Ireland

The NDNAD will expand as a result of changes to the law in Scotland. Unlike England and Wales, Scotland has not extended its inclusion regime to cover those charged but not convicted of an offence. Consequently, most samples and profiles taken in Scotland from suspects, and exported for speculative searching on the NDNAD, must be destroyed following a not-proven or not-guilty verdict in court. However, following the Scottish Executive instigated consultation 'Police retention of prints and samples: Proposals for legislation' in 2005, the retention regime in Scotland has undergone some changes. The Police, Public Order and Criminal Justice

(Scotland) Act 2006 allows the police to retain, for a limited period of time, DNA samples and profiles taken from suspects arrested or detained but not convicted, provided that criminal proceedings have been instituted against them for sexual or violent offences. In such cases the police are empowered to retain the sample and profiles for at least three years following the conclusion of judicial proceedings and may apply for an extension of such a retention for a further two years (there is no limit on the amount of two year extensions that may be granted).

This legislative arrangement produces a retention regime which depends upon the judicial route taken by defendants in Scotland's criminal justice system. For instance, if a suspect is arrested for assault and offered a fiscal fine or another non-court disposal the legislation requires that their DNA samples and profiles are destroyed (this applies to all non-court disposals in Scotland). However, if a defendant elects to go to trial and is subsequently found innocent their DNA samples and profiles can be retained.

A small increase in the NDNAD collection has also recently taken place when subject profiles currently held by the Forensic Science Service Northern Ireland (FSSNI) on behalf of the Police Service of Northern Ireland (PSNI) were first exported to the NDNAD following the acquisition of the required ISO accreditation by the FSSNI laboratory. In fact the NDNAD Annual Report 2005/2006 records the 'back-loading' of 36,219 subject profiles that had already been loaded on the Northern Ireland database prior to accreditation (although they are currently marked as 'pre-accredited' in order that 'the police were aware of their provenance'). Existing crime scene profiles have not been 'back-loaded' in this way.

'Roll back' v *'Universal'*

These are some of the ways in which the NDNAD may be expanded in the near future, albeit through relatively small incremental legislative, administrative and technical changes. Yet, of course, there are those who would wish to see a very different future for the database, namely a reduction in its permanent collection and a reformulation of police powers to use it. As we have argued elsewhere in this book, there are those, such as Genewatch UK, Liberty, individual lawyers, criminologists and geneticists, as well as a small number of MPs, who have persistently argued that profiles taken from those suspected but not subsequently convicted of a crime should be removed from any police database. While some of these agencies and individuals suggest that a growing database increases the danger of misleading investigations and misinforming judicial investigations by the spectre of false matching, others focus on the ways in which such an enlargement of state record keeping on those who have once been the attention of police interest alters the relationship between state and citizen in more general terms.

It is this latter spectre, of the transformation of a nation of citizens into a nation of suspects (or a transformation of significant numbers of them into a sub-nation of suspects), that seems to have resonated more widely among a range of expert and lay publics. At the time of writing, two important UK public bodies (the Nuffield Council on Bioethics, and the Human Genetics Commission) are engaged in consultation exercises to determine the degree of public support for the forensic DNA identification regimes that are described in this book. Furthermore, the Nuffield Council is pursuing its version of this exercise as part of a wider expert evaluation of the social and ethical implications of the widening police use of bioinformation in support of criminal investigation. While neither of these bodies has yet to produce a report or any policy recommendations, each is deliberating a common set of questions surrounding these practices, including the significance of the retention of genetic material from juvenile suspects and offenders, and the disproportionate representation of minority ethnic group DNA profiles on the NDNAD. It is widely recognised that figures for the loading and retention of profiles from juveniles and from minority ethic groups are simply a reflection of the ways in which such categories of individuals are policed in the UK, but it is also believed that the further inscription of the effects of these practices in the form of genetic databasing adds unacceptably to the ethical, social and political significance of these practices.

However, the prospect of 'rolling back' the database and the removal of a large number of profiles from it seems highly unlikely. This is, in part, explained by the way in which the database has become represented as an essential, and seemingly indispensable, technology in the contemporary focus on crime management. Regardless of its actual success in mundane policing (which, as we have argued, remains debateable), it is the *promise* of the database – the 'genetic imaginary' (Gelach 2005) of automated criminal detection – which forms the basis of a government-inspired discourse about this 'weapon' against crime. This discourse not only stresses the current success of the database but asserts the vital need to maximise its expansion and capacity for use continuously. So powerful has this discourse become in the last decade that it has been only partly subject to that other established technology of government – that of 'audit' and 'evidence-informed policy'. As we argued in Chapter 6, claims about the effectiveness of, for example, retaining profiles from those not convicted have not yet been subject to adequate examination. Nor was this issue raised during the various legal challenges to the retention of profiles from those not convicted of offences. On the contrary, in the final hearing of R v Marper and S (2004) it was asserted by the Law Lords: 'The more complete the database, the better the chance of detecting criminals, both those guilty of crimes past and those whose crimes are yet to be committed' (para. 88).

The current government position on the effectiveness of retaining profiles from the unconvicted is both contradictory and misleading. It is contradictory insofar as it simultaneously asserts the importance of this retention regime for the detection of serious crime (particularly crimes against the person), while also admitting that no official statistics are kept on the contribution that DNA profiling and the NDNAD make to the detection of such crimes. In a House of Commons written answer on the 1 March 2006, Hazel Blears, on behalf of the Secretary of State for the Home Department, wrote that:

Information on the number of serious crimes such as murder, manslaughter and rape that have been detected using DNA profiles taken from suspects who had previously been arrested, charged but not convicted of an offence is not collected by the Home Office as detections are achieved through integrated criminal investigation and not by forensic science alone.

In addition to this contradictory position on the significance of DNA profiling and databasing for the detection of serious crime, recently released government figures on the number of profiles retained on the NDNAD from individuals without convictions or cautions (those with no 'criminal records') have revealed this category of persons to be much larger than previously reported. While earlier in 2006 the Home Office had asserted that there were about 140,000 such individuals, a parliamentary answer by Joan Ryan on behalf of the Secretary of State for the Home Department revealed that in fact profiles from 1,139,445 individuals with no criminal record were held on the database on 14 July 2006. There are two important points to make about this admission. The first is simply that it means that only two-thirds of the 3,457,000 individuals on the NDNAD have been convicted or cautioned for a recordable offence, a fact that in itself may give pause for thought about any characterisation of the

NDNAD as a database of known suspect offenders. The second is that it encourages a very different interpretation of the significance of a figure provided within an answer to earlier Parliamentary questions answered on the 1 March 2006 and on the 9 October 2006. In the first of these answers, Hazel Blears stated that:

since the amendment to the Police and Criminal Evidence Act 1984 in May 2001 ... about 200,000 samples have been retained that would previously have had to be destroyed. From these, approximately 8,439 profiles of individuals have been linked with crime scene stains. (Hansard, 1 March 2006, Column 842)

In the second answer, Lynne Jones asserted that:

since April 2004 sampling persons who have been arrested but not proceeded against has yielded a match with a crime scene stain in over 3,000 offences. (Hansard, 9 October, Column 491)

While both 8,439 matches made to 200,000 unconvicted individuals, and 3,000 matches made to 140,000 unconvicted individuals, may already seem a small proportion, both can be seen to be vanishingly smaller when understood as a proportion of more than the 1.1 million profiles from unconvicted individuals whom the government has now revealed are held on the NDNAD.

Of course, despite the intricacies of whatever official statistics are available, in one sense the assertion by the Law Lords cited a few paragraphs earlier is correct: the larger the number of individuals whose profiles are held on any forensic DNA database, the greater the likelihood that profiles derived from crime scene stains will be matched when compared with this collection. However, this fails to address the question of what difference the inclusion of those who are not convicted makes to the detection of 'crimes past' or crimes 'yet to be committed'. Rather, the question is given little prominence within a criminal justice discourse which continually asserts that expanding the database automatically assures its greater success. What is interesting in England and Wales is that this view has attained such prominence that the possibility of reducing the range of categories of persons held on database is quickly dismissed by those who (like the former Prime Minister, Tony Blair) represent it as a 'vital way of fighting crime in the modern world'. It seems certain that unless a legal challenge succeeds in the European Court of Human Rights (and perhaps not even then) it is highly unlikely that the current government will alter its inclusion regime for the NDNAD. In fact one possible and unintended outcome of a successful legal challenge, based on an appeal against discrimination using Article 14 of the European Convention of Human Rights, is that the UK government could respond with plans for a universal database containing the profiles of the entire population.

Indeed, since the NDNAD came into existence in 1995 there has been continual speculation and concern about the possible extension of the collection to cover the entire population. There is no publicly stated government commitment to construct a universal DNA database and there is no official ACPO interest in having access to the DNA profiles of all individuals. Nevertheless, one of the most significant debates in recent years has been the question of creating a database containing profiles of every UK citizen. Such an idea was endorsed by Lord Sedley in his judgement of R *v* Marper and 'S' (2002), a view which he has subsequently expounded elsewhere (in the *London Review of Books*, 20 January 2005). In turn, worries about the possible trend towards a universal database are regularly expressed by human rights groups, parliamentarians, academics, and other commentators. A central preoccupation is the 'creeping' effect of legislation which year-by-year extends the database by affording the police greater powers to take, store, and search DNA profiles and samples. Liberty interprets these trends as examples of the government widening the database surreptitiously in ways which go beyond the reasonable objective of preventing and detecting crime. The idea of a universal DNA database would, for some, be a greater threat to liberty because of the potential uses (and misuses) to which it could be put. For others, such as Lord Sedley, it would remove the discrimination inherent in the current legislation.

Issues raised by a universal database are inevitably speculative since the government's consistent position is that such a database would not deliver worthwhile gains in the 'fight against crime'. Yet this position contrasts with other interested stakeholders, such as the Police Superintendents' Association (PSA), who have consistently expressed a desire for the creation of a population-wide database. The PSA most recently argued for a universal database in relation to the investigation and subsequent detection of Antoni Imiela, the so-called 'M25 rapist', who committed a series of rapes against women and girls. The basis for the PSA's argument is that a database match with the DNA profile obtained from the first of Imiela's victims would have served to identify Imiela as a suspect prior to at least seven subsequent attacks. However, this ignores that under current arrangements persons like Imelia *will* be present on the NDNAD: Imelia had been previously arrested and convicted of violent offences prior to the series of rapes but the timing of his conviction meant he was not present on the NDNAD (his last sentence, of 14 years imprisonment, ended in 1996, prior to the 'mopping up' exercise carried out by the Home Office).

No universal criminal database has ever existed in England and Wales and there would be staunch opposition to any proposal to create one. Yet there are those who argue for the creation of a national and universal DNA register, on the basis that it would actually enhance civil liberties rather than damage them. Alec Jeffreys, for instance, has consistently argued that the current composition and structure of the NDNAD is discriminatory because it contains a 'random' sample of innocent people. In his recent evidence to the UK Parliament Select Committee on Science and Technology he stated:

> I have repeatedly argued that I am totally opposed to the extension of the database. I regard it as highly discriminatory [because] you will be sampling excessively within ethnic communities, for example. The whole thing seems to be predicated on the assumption that the suspect population are people who would be engaged in future criminal behaviour. I have never seen any statistical justification for that assertion; none at all. Yes, it is discriminatory. I believe there has been one case that has gone to appeal and lost in the UK and has gone to the European Court of Justice. It will be extremely interesting to see their ruling on this.

Jeffreys' assertion that the database contains a significantly disproportionate representation of individuals from ethnic communities has subsequently been taken up by a number of other bodies, including Genewatch and the Human Genetics Commission. The NDNAD Annual Report has only included statistics on the ethnic appearance distribution of subject records since 2006, but in evidence given to the House of Commons Home Affairs Select Committee (2007: para 33), Baroness Scotland 'confirmed that three-quarters of the young black male population will soon be on the DNA database'. There is much more to say about this issue, but here we note only that it reveals the extent to which the NDNAD currently comprises a problematic collection of profiles which not only reflects existing forms of social differentiation, but may actually promote and promulgate discrimination. Somewhat ironically, we may see that the resolution to this problem, impelled through legal challenges, may not be a reduction of the database to hold only those convicted of recordable offences (which, after all, would still be disproportionate to the wider population in its ethnic composition) but, on the contrary, the creation of an even wider database of the entire population.

Data-sharing and exchange

Besides expanding the NDNAD as a discrete national collection there are both policy and policing ambitions to make the NDNAD inter-operable with other intelligence sources. There are three key ways in which this could be achieved:

- through more efficient 'joined-up' police record keeping in the UK;
- through co-joining the NDNAD to DNA databases in other jurisdictions to create either European or global coverage; and
- through the creation of mechanisms for data access to, and possible exchange with, non-forensic DNA databases.

Joined-up intelligence

The first possibility is already an explicit aim of both the current government and the police. The publication of the *Police Science and Technology Strategy 2003–2008* (Home Office 2003) demonstrates the Home Office's ambition to consolidate all existing, and potentially new, scientific instruments into an overall scheme to maximise the efficiency and effectiveness of investigations. The driving force of this ambition is to use more effective systems of data-sharing to enable more sophisticated intelligence gathering and use during an investigation. The issue here is not the enhanced collection of DNA samples from individual crime scenes or individuals, but the joining up of intelligence information within forces to aid criminal detection. The ambition is twofold: first, to systematically tie the full spectrum of intelligence material together so that it can be cross-referenced and checked; and second, to tie all forms of intelligence, to the individual to whom it relates. The emphasis is therefore not on the gathering of intelligence but on the arrangements for storing and analysing data once they are captured.

Perhaps the most widely discussed (and publicly contentious) idea for achieving this is through the introduction of ID or 'entitlement' cards. It seems likely that any ID card introduced into the UK will contain a biometric that can be used to prevent fraud and verify identity (Home Office 2002). An ID card scheme would function by providing a reference point to which a range of information would be tied. The effectiveness of the scheme would depend on a card's ability to capture individuality by means of a reliable and unique biometric identifier. Since DNA is the only biometric which is universal to all human beings it is extremely valuable for this purpose. The problems currently associated with obtaining, analysing, and verifying DNA make it unsuitable for inclusion on an ID card (whereas, as discussed above, Livescan technology now allows fingerprints to provide an almost instant method of ID verification). However, while it is unlikely in the short term that DNA will be used directly on ID cards, direct or indirect links to the NDNAD could play an important role in the intelligence systems developed in conjunction with this scheme.

Inter-operability and internationalisation

The second and most important form of database linkage relates to ambitions, and some existing measures, to allow data-sharing between forensic databases throughout Europe and the rest of the world. Current local arrangements within the UK highlight the success of data-sharing between England and Wales and Scotland to establish database coverage across the whole of Britain (see Johnson and Williams 2004). These arrangements currently allow police forces in each jurisdiction to share information in order that cross-border coverage can be maintained. The advantages in developing similar arrangements across, at the very least, Europe and, potentially, the whole globe are obvious in relation to international, cross-border crime: data-sharing is an important aspect of policing in mainland Europe and in all landmasses composed of multiple criminal justice jurisdictions.

The idea of international DNA database harmonisation has been embraced by Interpol who have heavily invested in the development and implementation of their own cross-national register of profiles. The Interpol DNA Gateway was set up at the Interpol General Secretariat in July 2003 and aims to provide a resource for DNA exchange and comparison between Interpol's 181 member countries. The database remains small despite Interpol's attempts to encourage its member states to submit profiles for the investigation of particular crimes or individuals. The Interpol database contains significant contributions from only two countries, Croatia and the UK, who have provided a number of unmatched crime scene profiles. This low submission rate to the database highlights, among a range of other factors, a general recognition that there are limited intelligence benefits to be gained in most crime investigation, by exporting large numbers of DNA profiles for international searching. Although the Interpol database acts as a hub for the exchange of intelligence information between police forces it has so far only recorded one 'hit' – between a newly entered profile from Slovenia and a previously entered profile from Croatia (nation states which together share both a border and a common policing history).

The long-standing European DNA Profiling Group – formed in 1988 to promote international standards in DNA profiling – reinforced by the later involvement of the European Network of Forensic Institutes has pursued an agenda for DNA profile sharing within the boundaries of the European Union. DNA profile exchange within the EU is now a significant political issue but is largely underdeveloped in terms of formal political agreement. A Council Resolution (2001/C 187/01) on the exchange of DNA analysis results between member states outlines procedures for the exchange of DNA profiles across the EU by police forces for the purposes of criminal investigations. However, there has been no significant EU legal instrument developed to specifically address or develop the use of DNA between member states or by EU organisations such as Europol.

What has developed in recent years has been the incorporation of discussions regarding DNA profile sharing into various wider EU 'security' plans and strategies. Often these strategies, such as the European Security Strategy 2003, combine international policing issues with more general security concerns, such as the control of borders. While these address separate concerns and attempt different solutions – for instance, border control issues have largely focused on immigration and have also been the focus of appropriate immigration authorities, while the investigation of trans-national crime remains a matter for policing – it is far from surprising that attempts to more effectively control borders are implicated with the policing and investigation of crime because both are relevant to particular problems (such as terrorism) and solutions to both often require a sharing of resources between the police and other state agencies.

An example of how an appeal to security subsumes both sets of issues is in the Hague Multi-annual Programme 2004 which now proposes 'Ten priorities for the next five years': in this programme security means both the effective control of borders and the rapid investigation and detection of crime. The Hague Programme proposes to extend biometric technologies as a means of regulating movement of persons into the EU. A practical example of this commitment is in the establishment of EU biometric passports containing fingerprints. Alongside this commitment to biometric passports have been discussions about the potential to utilise DNA profiling. One example of this commitment was expressed in a statement made at a recent meeting of the G5 in the UK by David Blunkett, then the UK's Home Secretary:

> Our discussions have given a real impetus to EU work on illegal immigration, border security and counter-terrorism. Terrorists and organised criminals do not respect borders and it is vital that we have effective laws, intelligence-led policing and close cross border co-operation to help us tackle international crime. The larger EU countries have a particular role to play in developing DNA and fingerprint databases and tracking systems and encouraging other member states to focus on key measures to help us share intelligence. [T]he collection and appropriate sharing of DNA and forensic material [is] crucial in monitoring the links of terrorist groups using cross border movement as a method of covering their tracks and avoiding detection.

What Blunkett asserts is that an essential feature of policing trans-national crime is the establishment of EU-wide DNA intelligence systems. As the quote shows, he emphasised two important elements about the use of DNA for security purposes in the EU: first, that all member states should establish national DNA collections and, second, the exchange of information between them should be increased.

This desire to foster greater sharing of DNA intelligence across the EU is just one element of a much broader and on-going agenda to enhance cooperation between law enforcement agencies within member states. Already in the EU there are various ways in which intelligence is exchanged for the purposes of law enforcement: these range from local interactions between police forces, the systematic exchange of information through systems such as Schengen, and the use of supra-national organisations such as Europol. However, there are plans to attempt to significantly enhance the exchange of intelligence. For instance, in 2004, following the Madrid bombing, the European Commission published a document entitled 'Towards Enhancing Access to Information by Law Enforcement Agencies'. The central aim expressed by the document was to find new ways of allowing greater access and flows of intelligence information between member states. Importantly, it proposes that central to these new mechanisms should be the 'principle of equivalent access' allowing every national and trans-national law enforcement authority in the EU to have the right to access any intelligence database held and operated by any member state. The ultimate aim is to achieve the 'free circulation of information between law enforcement authorities … [and overcome] the legal, technical and practical problems hindering exchange between Member States'. Similarly, the Hague Multi-annual Programme stresses the 'principle of availability' for data exchange between law enforcement agencies. With effect from 1 January 2008 and throughout the EU, a law enforcement officer in one member state can obtain any information needed from another law enforcement agency in another member state.

The principle of availability will affect the current arrangements and practices for exchanging DNA profiles across the EU. In relation to the practical sharing of such intelligence there are three types of DNA exchange which currently take place between member states. The first is the exchange of individual profiles between one or more law enforcement authorities for the purpose of casework. This, for example, could be sharing crime scene profiles in order to potentially link multiple crimes. Such an exchange is undertaken to link crime scenes to named suspects but does not involve the 'cold searching' of a database. A second type of exchange, which does involve cold searching, takes place when a law enforcement agency allows its DNA database to be speculatively searched by an agency from another member state. In such circumstances, the database might be searched using a crime scene profile obtained from outside its own jurisdiction. A third type of exchange involves the submission of profiles for storage and searching on supra-national databases. An example of this is the type of databasing currently operated by Europol and Interpol.

It is the second type of exchange which is now of most political interest in the EU. Initial discussions regarding a European DNA database were quickly subsumed by an interest in allowing law enforcement agencies in member states to have access to speculative search collections outside of their own jurisdiction. The advantage of this type of exchange is that it does not require legal or judicial harmonisation between member states. Instead, collections retain their national legal integrity but are made technically open to searching from profiles submitted from other jurisdictions. One significant development in this area has been the Prüm Convention signed by seven EU states (Austria, Belgium, France, Germany, Luxembourg,

The Netherlands and Spain) in May 2005. Prüm was not conceived as a European Union Convention but has since been incorporated into EU law. The convention outlines principles and procedures for the comprehensive exchange of a range of intelligence data between the law enforcement agencies of EU states. DNA profile exchange and database access are made a priority and Prüm proposes to allow the mutual automated access of member state's databases in order to facilitate speculative searching across national borders. Prüm is an important example of a number of bi-lateral agreements which are currently under discussion within the European Community to aid the transference of profile information between police forces. Yet a number of technological, legislative, and ethical problems are associated with the exchange of data in this way.

Technological problems have been debated since the late 1980s when a divergence of DNA profiling techniques produced remarkably different, and non-compatible, individual profiles. The range of STR profiling methods, analysing different combinations of loci, currently makes data-sharing across jurisdictions problematic. Interpol are concerned to implement a minimal universal standard of profiling so that individual profiles can more easily be loaded and searched on their DNA database. This ambition is far from realised because local differences in profiling are extensive. Nevertheless, there are sufficient and increasing similarities between STR systems across the world to allow data-sharing via Interpol. In the EU there is greater harmonisation since, throughout the 1990s, the European Network of Forensic Science Institutes consistently worked to promote the establishment of a core set of DNA markers across Europe. As a result there are seven STR loci common to all European laboratories, allowing exchange and comparison to take place between them. Furthermore, because some EU labs use the same multiplexes then exchange can proceed using a greater number of loci. Yet the current situation is far from resolved. The European Network of Forensic Science Institutes recently argued (2005) for additional common loci in all EU laboratories in order to increase the number of universal loci used from seven to ten. This is advocated on the basis of increasing statistical certainty of comparison.

A more important set of scientific issues, which are raised prior to the laboratory analysis of DNA, still pose a problem in the EU: this is the variation across member states in the collection and handling of DNA trace material at crime scenes. As the European Network of Forensic Science Institutes (ENFSI) notes: 'Crime scene management, examination procedures and standards vary widely between countries ... One of the benefits of internationally accepted guidance to good practice in crime scene examination would be the assurance that, if followed, the data derived from the evidence would not be compromised'. In other words, the variations in crime scene examination, and the collection, recording, and storage, of trace materials produce differences in the quality of materials subsequently submitted to laboratories. ENFSI recognises the importance of establishing international good practice for crime scene collection of DNA in order to ensure both parity in the quality of materials collected and the data subsequently produced from them. At the moment, the lack of international standards in this area raises significant 'quality control' issues in terms of international databasing and cross border exchange.

There are important legal issues raised by the exchange of data across national boundaries which have not been addressed in any government consideration of the potential for international DNA sharing or harmonisation. These issues relate to the ways in which, under existing arrangements for the exchange of intelligence material (particularly across Europe, subject to the Europol Convention), tensions are created by both domestic and EU legislation designed to ensure data protection and personal privacy. While DNA profiles can be divulged to those outside of England and Wales under exemptions in the Data Protection Act (1998) there has been no specific government consideration of this issue. Nor have guidelines been issued for the handling and exchange of DNA profiles other than those contained in the general provisions of the EU legislation under which an exchange is authorised (Title VI of the Treaty of the European Union) and the Europol Conventions which frame them (Title IV of the Europol Convention which outlines parameters for the storage and use of personal information). Given the repeated assertion from government and the Custodian of the NDNAD that public trust and confidence in the database are fundamental to its existence, the sharing of 'personal' data across national jurisdictions is highly significant. The process of exchanging DNA profiles across national borders means that, inevitably, information deemed as 'personal' leaves the jurisdiction in which it was obtained. Concerns have been expressed that when DNA profiles are submitted to police forces abroad there is little data protection legislation to prevent their unauthorised storage and use. Furthermore, there is no oversight body to monitor or assess the exchange of DNA profiles or any organisation to make enquiries and possible complaints to on behalf of individuals.

The legal basis for exchanging DNA profile information between member states is afforded by several treaties and conventions. The original 1959 Convention from the Council of Europe (which is not an EU institution but all EU states are members) established mutual assistance in criminal matters. The Maastricht Treaty contains the principles on which member states may exchange intelligence information for a range of policing purposes. In 2000, under the remit of Article 24 of the Treaty of the European Union, the Council adopted the 'Convention on Mutual Assistance in Criminal Matters between the Member States of the European Union'. The aim of this convention is to 'modernise' cooperation and to promote the 'spontaneous exchange of information' between member states. DNA exchange is not mentioned specifically in EU treaties but the Council of the European Union have made a number of recommendations regarding its exchange. In June 1997 the Council formally recommended the establishment of a network of compatible databases across the EU and, as a second step, an EU-wide database. In June 2001 the Council made further recommendations regarding the transmission of 'sensitive' DNA information between states. In pointing out that exchanging DNA profile information may reveal sensitive information about an individual (such as hereditary characteristics) the Council raised the issues of privacy and confidentiality.

The Council therefore recognised that the exchange of DNA between law enforcement agencies does raise significant issues regarding data protection. Yet the exchange of intelligence information between law enforcement agencies (both national and supranational) takes place in a complex environment of both local and EU data protection legislation. In 1995 the EU introduced a data protection directive. Directive 95/46/EC requires the establishment of common data protection authorities in all member states (it had to be implemented by 1998) to ensure that all member states observe the same data protection principles. It also requires that where data are exchanged between member states and 'third parties' (those outside the EU) such parties have in place suitable data protection systems. The outcome of the directive has been the establishment of data protection laws in each member state and an official body to oversee their implementation. However, such legislation remains variable in each nation state.

In relation to the exchange of personal information via international policing organisations established under either the first or third pillars of the EU – such as Europol or the Schengen Information System – national data protection legislation does not apply. What is applicable to the storage and use of personal information by such agencies is EU Regulation 45/2001, which established a Data Protection Supervisor to ensure data protection standards for information handled by all EU institutions. The Data Protection Supervisor's role remains problematic in relation to the exchange of DNA profiles because of significant exemptions that are made in EU law regarding the work of law enforcement agencies. The Supervisor does not have the authority to intervene with agencies such as Europol which are governed by their own conventions. As a result data-exchange takes place in a curious legislative 'space' between national data protection laws and a lack of international oversight and governance. The Data Protection Supervisor has recently issued a number of independent opinions on the increased exchange of information between member states which technically fall outside of its remit: for instance, in responding to proposals from the Council in 2004 to significantly change the exchange of criminal record information between member states the Data Protection Supervisor cited the European Convention of Human Rights.

Exploiting non-intelligence resources

There is a third way in which DNA profiling may be subject to police development in the future: that is, through the comparison of crime scene profiles with data held on non-forensic genetic databases. The concern that medical databases may be subject to police access is often raised as a significant threat to personal privacy. While it is rare for police to attempt to access genetic records held by the NHS or other health researchers, there has been at least one significant case where this has occurred. This involved the police gaining access to information derived from samples given voluntarily to a Medical Research Council study of HIV. Confidential information, revealing the HIV status of one Stephen Kelly, was used to convict him of recklessly passing the virus to his girlfriend, an Anne Craig. Police accessed medical records, using a warrant, which established a link between Craig's particular strain of the HIV virus and Kelly's. This case demonstrates the capacity for the police to utilise medical evidence in this way and their power to access it. For some this has provided a basis for arguing for greater legal restrictions on such powers and the rights of medical researchers to refuse the police access to information. For others, it suggests the need to include a reference to such potential access in initial consent forms.

However, it would be a mistake to over-estimate the usefulness that access of this kind would afford the police during most criminal investigations. Medical databases cannot be speculatively searched in the manner of the NDNAD due to the types of records that constitute them – DNA (STR) profiles are distinct to the NDNAD (although greater use of medical databases could result from the adoption of SNP profiling). Nor would there be any significant advantage in cross-referencing non-forensic databases with the NDNAD. One concern may be the potential for the police to access medical databases to identify an individual with a specific medical characteristic. This could be undertaken to obtain a list of possible suspects who share a medical trait identified from a crime scene sample. The utility use of medical databases for these purposes (which would be permitted by the law in England and Wales) is currently reduced by the capacity to analyse crime scene samples and the high volume and costly investigations of large groups of individuals that might be found on databases. Nevertheless, the establishment of UK Biobank, which will contain a large number of genetic samples, raises concerns about the adequacy of data protection and the level of confidentiality for the individuals concerned. UK Biobank has stated that it will allow access to information by the police only where a court-order is presented and under certain circumstances may even seek to resist such an order. Yet the HGC has expressed the view that access to such personal information, in the interests of both the success of projects such as UK Biobank and the confidentiality of individuals, should be blocked to the police and the courts.

Conclusion

Our aim in this chapter has been to outline some of the possible ways in which the NDNAD could develop in the future and to suggest some of the issues raised by these potential developments. It seems certain to us that the NDNAD expansion is not over and that new categories of persons will continue to be added to this heterogeneous collection of 'suspects'. Underpinning these possible developments is a range of further scientific innovations in DNA profiling technology which we consider in the final chapter of this book.

Note

1 Home Office Consultation: Modernising Police Powers: Review of the Police and Criminal Evidence Act (PACE) 1984.

Chapter 9

Conclusion

In the course of this book we have examined some of the ways in which the use of genetic information in criminal investigations has both contributed to and been shaped by the creation of a national DNA database. In particular, we have described a number of important scientific, technical, legislative and policy developments which have together transformed the forensic uses of DNA in England and Wales. Contemporary investigative practice in a large number of criminal jurisdictions now involves the increasingly routine search for DNA evidence at crime scenes and the collection of DNA samples from those suspected of involvement in criminal offences. While local regulations structure the circumstances under which such samples can be taken, used, and subsequently retained, the forensic use of DNA is a global phenomenon.

The UK's lead in this world-wide expansion in the forensic uses of DNA is based on a number of key legislative and policy initiatives which, harnessing and shaping important developments in science and technology, have rhetorically constructed and financially facilitated the NDNAD as a key tool in the detection and reduction of crime, especially volume crime. As we have argued throughout this book, at least four key changes have provided the basis for the ascendancy of DNA within policing. First, there was the redefinition of what constituted an intimate sample, which allowed the mass use of a simple and cheap collection technique (the buccal scrape) by police officers. Second, the criteria for NDNAD inclusion have been gradually expanded so that the database now contains any person arrested on suspicion of a recordable offence. Third, the law has changed to allow samples and profiles obtained from all suspects to be held indefinitely. Finally, a national funding programme supported by new forms of performance measurement has played a significant role in shaping police scientific support work and the subsequent population and uses of the NDNAD.

Yet it would be a mistake, in our view, to see this legislative and policy history in any simple linear form. Development of the NDNAD has not proceeded from or moved towards any clearly defined or hegemonic aims. Rather, legislative changes have been born out of proactive and reactive responses to arising situations within the criminal justice system, scientific and technological innovation, and from policing demands and practices. While it is arguable that the current government is now committed to an expanded database (and, more generally, to broad-based surveillance over a target population) this ambition was not prefigured in the original construction of this collection of genetic material. The current aim of government – to establish a database comprising a 'pool' of all 'active criminal suspects' – evolved from problems inherent in the legislative framework up until the 2001 Act, which gave authority for the retention (and retrospective retention) of profiles on the database of those who, being at one time criminal suspects, had been later exonerated of all charges. Yet, as a result, and within one decade since its introduction, we have witnessed the enactment of a series of legislative changes which have secured the capacity of the database to function as, what is now rhetorically called, a crucial 'weapon' against crime. The growth of the legislative framework to expand the database and empower the police to maximise its utilisation has been swift, and there has been strong public support for these developments.

None of this should negate the significance of the scientific and technical developments which underpin the NDNAD. The epistemic authority of molecular biology has been used to enhance police investigations through technical developments (such as the introduction of high-throughput screening, which makes the storage and analysis of DNA faster, easier and cheaper) that have in turn contributed to the transformation of what was once a complex and expensive bespoke laboratory procedure into a highly automated and routine analytical practice. It is important to acknowledge, as we have throughout this book, how important scientific developments are in reshaping the landscape in which operational policing takes place. At the time of writing a current review of PACE is considering legislative changes, which if implemented will further widen the scope of suspect sampling in England and Wales, on the basis that 'technological developments are moving rapidly which should enable more effective and efficient methods of gathering, retaining and making use of identification material'. It is the promise of these developments, and the high(er)-tech future they promise for policing, which provides a basis on which to drive forward further legislative and policy change.

For those concerned to promote the importance of DNA databasing within policing significant attention is always given to the seemingly spectacular success of the technology in 'solving' crime. For example, in a recent (2005) report evaluating the DNA Expansion Programme the Home Office made a number of claims about the effectiveness of the NDNAD in detecting offenders: it claimed the annual number of direct DNA detections was 19,873 in 2004/05 and in addition 15,732 crimes were detected as a result of further investigations linked to the original case in which DNA was recovered. This 'enhanced capability to detect serious crimes', the report argued, is based on an average monthly match rate of 3,000 (there were approximately 40,000 matches in 2004/05). Furthermore, it was argued that the database increases 'the ability to solve serious crimes' because 'serious offenders are often detected and caught because they are picked up and DNA sampled by the police at a later date for a relatively minor offence'. We assessed these and other statistical claims in Chapter 6 and noted the way in which they are deployed by government to promote the database as vital in the intelligence 'armoury' used in the 'fight against crime'. Yet we also noted the problematic nature of such statistics and their failure to elucidate the complexity of the contribution of the NDNAD in crime management.

In thinking about the importance of the NDNAD within the criminal justice systems of the UK we focused on its entrenched status as an intelligence, rather than evidential, resource. We noted that in the UK the fact that a match made via the database between a crime scene sample profile and the subject sample profile of the accused is not revealed to a jury. Nevertheless, it would be wrong to think that the existence of automated NDNAD comparison, and the matches they make, does not impact upon the whole of the criminal justice system. Some commentators have pointed out that the deployment of intelligence-led crime management strategies produces a range of negative effects upon due process. Gerlach (2005), for example, commenting upon the latest measures in Canada to compulsorily sample a wider range of suspects and those already convicted, argues that DNA databasing is significantly diminishing a number of due process principles:

DNA evidence and the DNA sampling of convicted offenders are having an instrumentalizing effect on crime management; there is a trend toward applying instrumental rationality over value rationality, and as a result, forensic DNA techniques are trumping legal protections for the accused. This instrumental rationality manifests itself not only in judicial decisions but also in police tactics for acquiring DNA evidence, in government policies, and in the increasing privatization of the DNA testing industry. (Gerlach 2005: 177)

Gerlach suggests that DNA profiling, rather than being a neutral or passive instrument of crime management practices such as intelligence-led policing, actually impels, increases and fashions the application of such practices and their associated values across the criminal justice system as a whole. As a result, he suggests, new forms of instrumental rationality come to replace the types of rationality which are the traditional foundations of due legal process. Such instrumental rationality is, he contends, already visible across the criminal justice system: in courtrooms where DNA, along with other forms of scientific evidence, reconfigure the objective of a trial so that the production of 'fairness' is replaced by the production of 'truth'; in the growth of new police tactics in surveillance where DNA profiling allows investigators to carry out mass screens of large numbers of innocent individuals (something which Gans (2001) has referred to as 'request surveillance') and which erodes their civic rights; and through the importation of values from the private sector (efficiency, profitability, productivity, and entrepreneurialism) which become the main ends of the criminal justice process. For Gerlach, these changes amount to a fundamental re-emphasis in the criminal justice system where the due process concern with 'justice' is overshadowed by the principles of crime management; management both of socially problematic individuals and their fiscal cost to the state. This, he argues, represents:

a shift in legal regimes away from an ideal type based on political value about the relationship between the individual and the state toward one based on values imported from the technological, scientific, and corporate domains. (Gerlach 2005: 91)

One fundamental effect of this shift is that 'the rituals of justice are now increasingly being performed behind laboratory doors instead of on the public stage of the court rooms' (2005: 8). For Gerlach, as well as a number of other commentators, this move towards 'genetic justice' is problematic because it is administered by agents of crime management with no concern for due process; in other words, DNA profiling and databasing are tools employed to code and survey a population for the purposes of policing and controlling risk.

This understanding of DNA intelligence does not view it simply as the first stage in a sequence of due process which ends with the presentation of DNA evidence in court. Rather, it comprehends the use of DNA profiling at these two sites as connected but relatively independent. In other words, DNA intelligence databasing in the UK does not rely on judicial authority at the point of its use nor are its results subject to judicial scrutiny. While DNA evidence is presented in court to support prosecutions, and while such evidence may (or may not) be the result of initial intelligence produced using the NDNAD, the court does not have access to the ways in which DNA profiling was employed to identify and apprehend suspects nor how the intelligence was used prior to the trial (for instance, during the interviewing of suspects by the police). Some commentators (e.g. McCartney 2006a, 2006b) see this situation as exemplifying an uncritical confidence in forensic identification techniques which in turn is leading to inadequate interrogation of the results derived from their applications to support criminal prosecutions.

Although it is easy to see why some would argue with such vehemence about the encompassing effects of DNA profiling and databasing on the criminal justice system – after all, as we have argued, DNA has quickly established itself as an epistemic authority for the adjudication of 'truth' in both police work and in court – the negative aspects are perhaps overplayed or presented in a solipsistic manner. After all, such arguments are in sharp contrast to claims about the impact of DNA upon the criminal justice process in terms of its spectacular capacity to introduce new standards of impartiality and objectivity. The potential of DNA, to both exculpate as well as inculpate suspects, has long been promoted as a method of improving the experience of suspects at the stage of both criminal investigation by the police and during prosecution in court. While there are those who imagine DNA as an unchallengeable 'witness' (Blake 1989) that overrides all other forms of either expert or lay testimony in court, there is in fact very little evidence to support claims that DNA leads to miscarriages of justice or a substantial diminution of legal safeguards in court. Nor is there any empirical research to support claims that DNA intelligence is inducing (false) admissions of guilt from suspects which some argue may lead to wrongful convictions in court.

As we argued in earlier, there are several issues about the need to clearly and fairly present DNA evidence in court. There is also the importance of establishing appropriate laboratory standards, reliable crime scene collection techniques, and standards in relation to database governance, so that police intelligence that *could* contribute to the prosecution of suspects is reliable. Yet the notion that DNA intelligence (or any intelligence-led policing) *necessarily* impacts upon due process in a negative way must be tempered by recognition of the benefits of the clear separation between DNA intelligence used in investigations and DNA evidence used in court. While some commentators see such a separation as detrimental to due criminal process it might also be argued that it provides a number of safeguards for criminal suspects, not least because the absence of database intelligence in court preludes a jury's awareness of a suspect's prior presence on the database.

Furthermore, it is precisely these criticisms about the failure to employ DNA intelligence at the early stages of criminal investigation which have provoked accusations of miscarriages of justice at the trail stage. Such criticisms have proved decisive in introducing schemes designed to aid those who seek post-conviction testing as a means of establishing their innocence. One such scheme is the Innocence Project in the USA which makes DNA profiling available to those individuals convicted and imprisoned of offences for which DNA was not used either during the original criminal investigation or at trial. While the USA has witnessed many more post-conviction exonerations than the UK (Johnson and Williams 2004b), and while such exonerations constitute a minor outcome in comparison to the number of convictions assured through the technology, it is still important to recognise the exculpatory power of DNA. When such exonerations occur, as Rothstein argues, they may indicate 'deeper structural problems in the criminal justice system' and may reveal prior trial errors based on 'faulty eyewitness testimony ... coerced or false confessions, or perjurious testimony by prison inmates' (Rothstein 2005: 2667).

At the very least we must recognise that the potential effects of DNA profiling and databasing on due criminal process can be both negative and enhancing. And, importantly, that these effects are not always the outcome of using DNA for the purposes of intelligence-led policing. This is not to deny the important social, legal and ethical issues which are raised by current police use of DNA. Nor is it to overplay the capacity of DNA, as in some representations used by both the Home Office and ACPO, to make 'automatic detections' or produce 'remote eliminations'. Yet in order to evaluate both the development of genetic intelligence databasing and its importance within policing it is crucial to separate an understanding of the role of such a database from the use of DNA profiling in court. If intelligence-led policing is driven by the production of suspects then the NDNAD is a means of such production; it is the 'engine' through which information is collated, harmonised and processed in order to produce intelligence. The fact that such an engine can run automatically, quickly, and continuously has impelled parliament to enact a series of the most significant changes in the criminal law to allow the police to maximise the population of the database.

Finally, there remain many policy questions concerning the use of DNA and the NDNAD for crime investigation. These range in scope, but include:

- whether the use of the NDNAD sustains, or even enhances asserted inequities in the criminal justice system;
- under what circumstances may those convicted be allowed to reopen cases to seek exoneration by DNA analysis;
- the relationship between DNA profiling, 'double jeopardy' and 'statutes of limitation';
- how the public accountability of the custodians and users of the NDNAD is assured; and
- what privacy rights are attached to information potentially recoverable from biological materials held by the laboratories that supply profiles to the NDNAD?
- what uses of these biological materials should be allowed?

These questions will not only structure future research on the NDNAD but should provide the foundations for debates about the significant social, ethical and legal issues which are raised by the operation of this increasingly important police resource.

References

Abaz, J., Walsh, S., Curran, J.M., Moss, D.S., Cullen, J., Bright, J-A., Crowe, G., Cockerton, S.L. and Power, T.E.B. (2002) 'Comparison of the variables affecting the discovery of DNA from common drinking containers', *Forensic Science International*, 126: 233–40.

Allen, R. and Redmayne, M. (1997) 'Bayesianism and juridical proof', *Evidence and Proof*, 1 (6).

Amey, P., Hale, C. and Uglow, S. (1996) *Proactive Policing*. Edinburgh: Scottish Central Research Unit.

Ashworth, A. (1998) *The Criminal Process: An Evaluative Study* (2nd edn). Oxford: Oxford University Press.

ACPO/FSS/Audit Commission (1996) *Using Forensic Science Effectively*. London: HMSO.

Association of Chief Police Officers (ACPO) (2004) *Investigation of Volume Crime Manual*. London: Association of Chief Police Officers.

Association of Chief Police Officers (ACPO) (2005) *DNA Good Practice Manual*. London: Association of Chief Police Officers.

Attorney General's Reference No. 3 (1999) 'Opinion of the Lords of Appeal for Judgement in the Cause, Attorney General's Reference No. 3 of 1999', on December 2000, House of Lords, London.

Audit Commission (1991) *Reviewing the Organisation of Provincial Police Forces*. London: Audit Commission.

Audit Commission (1993) *Helping With Enquiries: Tackling Crime Effectively*. London: HMSO.

Ball, K. (2005) 'Organisation, Surveillance and the Body: Towards a Politics of Resistance', *Organization*, 12: 89–108.

Barrow, K. (2005) *Study into Forensic Intelligence Packages: Process Flow Case Study*. London: Home Office.

Barton, A. and Evans, R. (1999) *Proactive Policing on Merseyside Police*. London: Home Office.

Bereano, P.L. (1992) 'The impact of DNA-based identification systems on civil liberties', in P.R. Billings (ed.), *DNA On Trial: Genetic Identification and Criminal Justice*. New York: Cold Spring Harbour Laboratory Press, pp. 119–28.

Beyleveld, D. (1997) 'Ethical issues in the forensic applications of DNA analysis', *Forensic Science International*, 88: 3–15.

Bieber, F. (2004) 'Science and technology of forensic DNA profiling: current use and future directions', in D. Lazer (ed.), *DNA and the Criminal Justice System*. Harvard: MIT Press.

Blake, E.T. (1989) 'Scientific and legal issues raised by DNA analysis', in J. Ballantyne, G. Sensabaugh and J. Witowski (eds), *DNA Technology and Forensic Science*. New York: Cold Spring Harbor Laboratory Press.

Blakey, D. (2002) 'Under the microscope refocused'. Paper presented at the Scientific Support Managers Conference, West Mercia, 12 June.

Braithwaite, J. (2000) 'The new regulatory state and the transformation of criminology', *British Journal of Criminology*, 40: 222–38.

Bright, J. and Petricevic, S.F. (2004) 'Recovery of trace DNA and its application to DNA profiling of shoe insoles', *Forensic Science International*, 145: 7–12.

Britton, P. (1998) *The Jigsaw Man*. London: Corgi.

Britton, P. (2001) *Picking Up the Pieces*. London: Corgi.

Brownlee, I. (1998) 'Taking DNA samples without consent from mentally disordered offenders: the impact of Home Office Circular 27/1997', *The Journal of Forensic Psychiatry*, 9: 413–23.

Buckleton, J. and Gill, P. (2005) 'Low copy number', in J. Buckleton, C.M. Triggs, and S.J. Walsh (eds), *Forensic DNA Evidence Interpretation*. London: CRC Press, pp. 257–97.

Butler, J. (1997) *Excitable Speech: A Politics of the Performative*. London: Routledge.

Callen, C.R. (1997) 'Inference from the secondary evidence of ordinary witnesses and scientific experts 2', in J.F. Nijboer and J.M. Reijntjes (eds.), *Proceedings of the First World Conference on New Trends in Criminal Investigation and Evidence*. Lelystad: Konninklijke Vermande.

Canter, D. (1995) *Criminal Shadows*. London: HarperCollins.

Caplan, J. and Torpey, J. (eds) (2001) *Documenting Individual Identity: The Development of State Practices in the Modern World*. Princeton: Princeton University Press.

Chakraborty, R., Stivers, D.N., Su, B., Zhong, Y. and Budowle, B. (1999) 'The utility of short tandem repeat loci beyond human identification: implications for development of new DNA typing systems', *Electrophoresis*, 20: 1682–96.

Cho, M.K. and Sankar, P. (2004) 'Forensic genetics and ethical, legal and social implications beyond the clinic', *Nature Genetics Supplement*, 36: S8–S12.

Cho, M.K. and Sankar, P. (2005) 'In reply to Shriver, Frudakis and Budowle', *Nature Genetics*, 36: 450–1.

Clarke, J., Gerwitz, S. and McLaughlin, E. (2000) *New Managerialism, New Welfare*. Buckingham: Open University Press.

CM. 2850 (1995) *Standards in Public Life: The First Report of the Committee on Standards in Public Life*. London: HMSO.

CM. 3179 (1996) *Spending Public Money: Governance and Audit Issues*. London: HMSO.

CM. 3557 (1997) *The Governance of Public Bodies: A Progress Report*. London: HMSO.

Cockerton, S.L. and Power, T.E.B. (2002) 'Comparison of the variables affecting the discovery of DNA from common drinking containers', *Forensic Science International*, 126: 233–40.

Cohen, S. (1985) *Visions of Social Control: Crime, Punishment and Classification*. Cambridge: Polity Press.

Cole, S. (2001) *Suspect Identities: A History of Fingerprinting and Criminal Identification*. Cambridge, MA: Harvard University Press.

Coleman, H. and Swenson, E. (1994) *DNA In the Courtroom: A Trial Watcher's Guide*. Seattle: Genelux Press.

Coulter, J. (1989) *Mind in Action*. Cambridge: Polity Press.

Damaska, M. (1973) 'Evidentiary barriers to conviction and two models of criminal procedure: a comparative study', *University of Pennsylvania Law Review*, 121: 506.

Darwin, L. (1914) 'The Habitual Criminal', *The Eugenics Review*, 6 (4): 204–18.

Dean, M. (1999) *Governmentality: Power and Rule in Modern Society*. London: Sage.

Duff, P. (1998) 'Crime control, due process and "The Case for the Prosecution"', *British Journal of Criminology*, 38: 611–15.

Duster, T. (2003) *Backdoor to Eugenics* (2nd edn). New York: Routledge.

Duster, T. (2004) 'Selective arrests, an ever-expanding DNA forensic database, and the specter of an early-twenty-first century equivalent of phrenology', in D. Lazer (ed.), *DNA and the Criminal Justice System: The Technology of Justice*. Cambridge, MA: MIT Press.

Duster, T. (2005) 'Race and Reification in Science', *Science*, 307: 1050–51.

Edmond, G. (2000) 'Judicial representations of scientific evidence', *Modern Law Review*, 63: 216–51.

Ericson, R.V. (1993) *Making Crime: A Study of Detective Work*. Toronto: University of Toronto Press.

Ericson, R.V. and Shearing, C.D. (1986) 'The scientification of police work', in G. Bohme and N. Stehr (eds), *The Knowledge Society: The Growing Impact of Scientific Knowledge on Social Relations*. Dordrecht: Reidel, pp. 129–59.

Ericson, R.V. and Haggerty, K.D. (1997) *Policing the Risk Society*. Oxford: Oxford University Press.

Evett, I.W. and Weir, B.S. (1998) *Interpreting DNA Evidence: Statistical Genetics for Forensic Scientists*. Sunderland, MA: Sinauer.
Evett, I.W., Gill, P.D., Lambert, J.A., Oldroyd, R., Frazier, S., Watson, S., Panchal, S., Connolly, A. and Kimnpton, C. (1997) 'Statistical analysis of data for three British ethnic groups from a new STR multiplex', *International Journal of Legal Medicine*, 110: 5–9.
Evett, I.W., Pinchin, R. and Buffery, C. (1992) 'An investigation of the feasibility of inferring ethnic origin from DNA profiles', *Journal of the Forensic Science Society*, 32: 301–6.

Findlay, I. (1988) 'Single cell PCR', in Y.M.D. Lo (ed.), *Methods in Molecular Medicine*. Towota, NJ: Humana Press.
Findlay, I., Taylor, A., Quirke, P., Frazier, R. and Urquhart, A. (1997) 'DNA fingerprinting from single cells', *Nature*, 389: 555–6.
Foreman, L.A., Smith, A.F.M. and Evett, I.W. (1997) 'Bayesian analysis of DNA profiling in forensic identification applications', *Journal of the Royal Statistical Society*, 160: 429–69.
Forensic Science Service (FSS) (1994) *Scenes of Crime Handbook*. London: The Forensic Science Service.
Forensic Science Service (FSS) (2000) *Memorandum of Understanding Between the Association of Chief Police Officers and the Custodian of the National DNA Database*. Birmingham: The Forensic Science Service.
Forensic Science Service (FSS) (2003) *Scenes of Crime Handbook*. London: The Forensic Science Service.
Forensic Science Service (FSS) (2004) *National DNA Database Annual Report 2003–2004*. London: HMSO.
Foucault, M. (1972) *The Archaeology of Knowledge*. London: Tavistock.
Foucault, M. (1977) *Discipline and Punish: The Birth of the Prison*. Harmondsworth: Penguin.
Foucault, M. (1979) 'Governmentality', *Ideology and Consciousness*, 6.
Freeman, M. and Reece, H. (eds) (1998) *Science in Court*. Aldershot: Ashgate.
Frudakis, T. *et al.* (2003) 'A classifier for the SNP-based inference of ancestry', *Journal of Forensic Sciences*, 48: 771–82.
Fujimura, J.H. and Fortun, M. (1996) 'Constructing knowledge across social worlds', in L. Nader (ed.), *Naked Science: Anthropological Inquiry into Boundaries, Power and Knowledge*. New York: Routledge.

Gans, J. (2001) 'Something to hide: DNA databases, surveillance and self-incrimination', *Current Issues in Criminal Justice*, 13: 168–84.
Garland, D. (1996) 'The limits of the sovereign state: strategies of crime control in contemporary society', *British Journal of Criminology*, 36: 445–71.
Garland, D. (2001) *The Culture of Control: Crime and Social Order in Contemporary Society*. Oxford: Oxford University Press.
Genewatch UK (2005) *The Police National DNA Database: Balancing Crime Detection, Human Rights and Privacy*. Bixton: Genewatch.

Gerlach, N. (2004) *The Genetic Imaginary: DNA in the Canadian Criminal Justice System*. Toronto: University of Toronto Press.

Gibson, M. (2001) 'The truth machine: polygraphs, popular culture and the confessing body', *Social Semiotics*, 11: 61–73.

Gieryn, T.F. (1999) *Cultural Boundaries of Science: Credibility on the Line*. Chicago: Chicago University Press.

Gill, P. (2000) *Rounding Up the Usual Suspects*. Aldershot: Ashgate.

Gill, P. (2001) 'An assessment of the utility of single nucleotide polymorphisms (SNPs) for forensic purposes', *International Journal of Legal Medicine*, 114: 204–10.

Gill, P., Jeffreys, A.J. and Werrett, D.J. (1985) 'Forensic application of DNA "fingerprints"', *Nature*, 318: 577–79.

Gill, P., Werrett, D.J., Budowle, B. and Guerrieri, R. (2004) 'An assessment of whether SNPs will replace STRs in national DNA databases', *Science and Justice*, 44: 51–5.

Ginzburg, C. (1980) 'Morelli, Freud and Sherlock Holmes: clues and scientific method', *History Workshop Journal*, 9: 5–36.

Ginzburg, C. (1983) 'Morelli, Freud and Sherlock Holmes: clues and scientific method', in U. Eco and T.A. Sebeok (eds), *The Sign of Three: Dupin, Holmes, Peirce*. Bloomington: Indiana University Press, pp. 81–118.

Ginzburg, C. (1990) 'Clues: roots of an evidential paradigm', in *Myths, Emblems, Clues*. London: Hutchinson, pp. 96–125.

Giusti, A., Baird, M. *et al.* (1986) 'Application of deoxyribonucleic acid (DNA) polymorphisms to the analysis of DNA recovered from sperm', *Journal of Forensic Science*, 31: 409–17.

Greeley, H.T., Riordan, D.P., Garrison, N.A. and Mountain, J.L. (2006) 'Family ties: the use of DNA offender databases to catch offenders', *Journal of Law, Medicine and Ethics*, 34: 248–62.

Green, R. (2007) 'Forensic investigation in the UK', in T. Newburn, T. Williamson and A. Wright (eds), *Handbook of Criminal Investigation*. Cullompton: Willan, pp. 338–56.

Grimes, E.A., Noake, P., Dixon, L. and Urquhart, A. (2001) 'Sequence polymorphism in the human melanocortin 1 receptor gene as an indicator of the red hair phenotype', *Forensic Science International*, 122: 124–29.

Guillén, M., Lareu, M.L., Pestoni, C., Salas, A. and Carracedo, A. (2000) 'Ethical-legal problems of DNA databases in criminal investigation', *Journal of Medical Ethics*, 26: 266–71.

Haggerty, K.D. and Ericson, R.V. (2000) 'The surveillant assemblage', *British Journal of Sociology*, 51 (4): 605–22.

Haggerty, K.D. and Ericson, R.V. (eds) (2006) *The New Politics of Surveillance and Visibility*. Toronto: University of Toronto Press.

Haimes, E. (2006) 'Social and ethical issues in the use of familial searching in forensic investigations', *Journal of Law, Medicine and Ethics*, 34: 263–76.

Heaton, R. (2000) 'The prospects for intelligence-led policing: some historical and quantitative considerations', *Policing and Society*, 9: 337–56.

Hebenton, B. and Thomas, T. (1995) *Policing Europe: Cooperation, Conflict and Control*. London: St Martin's Press.

Her Majesty's Inspectorate of Constabulary (HMIC) (1997) *Policing With Intelligence: Criminal Intelligence: A Thematic Inspection of Good Practice.* London: Home Office.

Her Majesty's Inspectorate of Constabulary (HMIC) (1998) *What Price Policing? A Study of Efficiency and Value for Money in the Police Service.* London: Home Office.

Her Majesty's Inspectorate of Constabulary (HMIC) (2000) *Under the Microscope: Thematic Inspection Report on Scientific and Technical Support.* London: Home Office.

Her Majesty's Inspectorate of Constabulary (HMIC) (2001) *Going Local: The BCU Inspection Handbook.* London: Home Office.

Her Majesty's Inspectorate of Constabulary (HMIC) (2002) *Getting Down to Basics: Emerging Findings from BCU Inspections in 2001.* London: Home Office.

Herber, B. and Herold, K. (1998) 'DNA typing of human dandruff', *Journal of Forensic Science*, 43: 648–56.

Higgs, E. (2001) 'The rise of the information state: the development of central state surveillance of the citizen in England 1500–2000', *Journal of Historical Sociology.* 14: 175–97.

Hill, R. (2007) 'Reflections on cot death cases', *Medicine, Science and the Law*, 47: 2–6.

Holmes, H.B. (1994) 'DNA fingerprints and rape: a feminist assessment', *Policy Sciences*, 27: 221–45.

Home Office (1988) *Annual Report of the Director.* Aldermaston: Home Office.

Home Office (1992) *Police Reform: A Police Service for the Twenty First Century*, London: Home Office.

Home Office (2002) *Entitlement Cards and Identity Fraud: A Consultation Paper.* London: Home Office.

Home Office (2003) *Police Science and Technology Strategy 2003–2008.* London: Home Office.

Home Office (2006) *DNA Expansion Programme 2000–2005: Reporting Achievement.* London: Home Office.

Home Office (2007) *The National DNA Database Annual Report 2005–2006.* London: Home Office.

House of Commons Home Affairs Select Committee (2007) *Young Black People and the Criminal Justice System.* London: HMSO.

House of Commons Select Committee on Science and Technology (2005), *Forensic Science On Trial.* London: HMSO.

House of Lords Select Committee on Science and Technology (1993) *Forensic Science. 5th Report HL Paper 24, Session 1992–3.* London: HMSO.

House of Lords Select Committee on Science and Technology (2001) *Human Genetic Databases: Challenges and Opportunities.* London: HMSO.

Human Genetics Commission (2001) *Whose Hands on your Genes? A Discussion Document on the Storage Protection and Use of Genetic Information.* London: HGC.

Hutchby, I. (2001) 'Technologies, texts and affordances', *Sociology*, 35 (2): 441–56.

Innes, M. (2001) 'Control creep', *Sociological Research Online*, 6 (3). Available at: www.socresonline.org.uk/6/3/innes.html.

Innes, M. (2003) *Understanding Social Control.* Maidenhead: Open University Press.

Innes, M., Fielding, N. and Cope, N. (2005) '"The appliance of science": the theory and practice of criminal intelligence analysis', *British Journal of Criminology*, 45: 39–57.

Jasanoff, S. (1995) *Science at the Bar: Law, Science and Technology in America.* Cambridge, MA: Harvard University Press.

Jasanoff, S. (1998) 'Witnessing DNA in the Simpson trial', *Social Studies of Science*, 28: 713–40.

Jasanoff, S. (2001) 'Science and law', *International Encylopedia of the Social and Behavioural Sciences.* New York: Elsevier.

Jasanoff, S. (2004) 'DNA's identity crisis', in D. Lazer (ed.), *DNA and the Criminal Justice System.* Harvard: MIT Press.

Jasanoff, S. (ed.) (2004) *States of Knowledge: The Co-production of Science and Social Order.* London: Routledge and Kegan Paul.

Jeffreys, A.J., Wilson, V., Neumann, R. and Keyte, J. (1988) 'Amplification of human minisatellites by polymerase chain reaction: towards DNA fingerprinting of single cells', *Nucleic Acids Research*, 16: 10953–71.

Jeffreys, A.J., Wilson, V. and Thein, S.L. (1985a) 'Hypervariable "minisatellite" regions in human DNA', *Nature*, 314: 67–73.

Jeffreys, A.J., Wilson, V. and Thein, S.L. (1985b) 'Individual-specific "fingerprints" of human DNA', *Nature*, 316: 76–9.

Jobling, M.A. (2001), 'Y-chromosomal SNP haplotype diversity in forensic analysis', *Forensic Science International*, 118: 158–62.

Jobling, M.A. and Tyler-Smith, C. (1995) 'Fathers and sons: the Y-chromosome and human evolution', *Trends in Genetics*, 11: 449–56.

Jobling, M.A., Pandya, A. and Tyler-Smith, C. (1997) 'The Y-chromosome in forensic analysis and paternity testing', *International Journal of Legal Medicine*, 110: 118–24.

John, T. and Maguire, M. (2003) 'Rolling out the National Intelligence Model: key challenges', in K. Bullock and N. Tilley (eds), *Essays in Problem-oriented Policing.* Cullompton: Willan, pp. 38–68.

Johnson, P. and Williams, R. (2004a) 'DNA and crime investigation: Scotland and the 'UK National DNA Database', *Scottish Journal of Criminal Justice*, 10: 71–84.

Johnson, P. and Williams, R. (2004b) 'Post-conviction DNA testing: the UK's first exoneration case?', *Science and Justice*, 4: 77–82.

Johnson, P., Martin, P. and Williams, R. (2003) 'Genetics and forensics: a sociological history of the National DNA Database', *Science Studies*, 16: 22–37.

Jones, C.A.G. (1994) *Expert Witnesses: Science, Medicine and the Practice of Law*. Oxford: Clarendon Press.

Jordan, K. and Lynch, M. (1998) 'The dissemination, standardisation and routinization of a molecular biological technique', *Social Studies of Science*, 28: 773–800.

Kaluszynski, M. (2001) 'Republican identity: bertillonage as government technique', in J. Caplan and J. Torpey (eds), *Documenting Individual Identity: The Development of State Practices in the Modern World*. Princeton: Princeton University Press.

Kellie, D.L. (2001), 'Justice in the age of technology: DNA and the criminal law', *Altern. Law Journal*, 26: 173–6.

Kennedy, H. (2004) *Just Law*. London: Chatto and Windus.

King, M. (1981) *The Framework of Criminal Justice*. London: Croom Helm.

Kirk, P.L. (1963) 'The Ontogeny of Criminalistics', *Criminology and Police Science*, 54: 235–42.

Knorr-Cetina, K.D. (1981) *The Manufacture of Knowledge: An Essay on the Constructivist and Contextual Nature of Science*. Oxford: Pergamon Press.

Latour, B. (1987) *Science in Action*. Milton Keynes: Open University Press.

Lazer, D. (ed.) (2004) *DNA and the Criminal Justice System: The Technology of Justice*. Cambridge, MA: MIT Press.

Lazer, D. and Meyer, M. (2004) 'DNA and the criminal justice system: consensus and debate', in D. Lazer (ed.), *DNA and the Criminal Justice System: The Technology of Justice*. Cambridge, MA: MIT Press.

Lincoln, P.J. (1997) 'Criticisms and concerns regarding DNA Profiling', *Forensic Science International*, 88: 23–31.

Loader, I. (2004), 'Policing, securitisation and democratisation in Europe', in T. Newburn and R. Sparks (eds), *Criminal Justice and Political Cultures: National and International Dimensions of Crime Control*. Cullompton: Willan.

Lombroso, C. (1876) *On Criminal Man*. Milan: Hoepli.

Lowe, A., Murray, C., Whitaker, J., Tully, G. and Gill, P. (2002) 'The propensity of individuals to deposit DNA and secondary transfer of low level DNA from individuals to inert surfaces', *Forensic Science International*, 129: 25–34.

Lowe, A.L., Urquhart, A., Foreman, L.A. and Evett, I.W. (2001) 'Inferring ethnic origin by means of an STR profile', *Forensic Science International*, 119: 17–22.

Lynch, M. (1998) 'The discursive production of uncertainty: the OJ Simpson Dream Team and the sociology of knowledge machine', *Social Studies of Science*, 28: 829–68.

Lynch, M. (2003) 'God's signature: DNA profiling, the new gold standard in forensic science', *Endeavour*, 27 (2): 93–7.

Lynch, M.D. and Jasanoff, S. (eds) (1998) *Contested Identities: Science, Law and Forensic Practice* (Special Issue of *Social Studies of Science*, Volume 28).

Lyon, D. (1991) 'Bentham's Panopticon: from moral architecture to electronic surveillance', *Queen's Quarterly*, 98 (3): 596–617.

Lyon, D. (2001) *Surveillance Society: Monitoring Everyday Life*. Buckingham: Open University Press.

Lyon, D. (2003) *Surveillance after September 11*. Cambridge: Polity Press.

Lyon, D. (ed.) (2006) *Theorizing Surveillance: The Panopticon and Beyond*. Cullompton: Willan.

Lyon, D. and Zureik, E. (eds) (1996) *Computers, Surveillance and Privacy*. Minneapolis: University of Minnesota Press.

Maguire, M. and John, T. (1995) *Intelligence, Surveillance and Informants: Integrated Approaches*. London: Home Office.

Manning, P.K. (1977) *Police Work: The Social Organisation of Policing*. Cambridge, MA: MIT Press.

Martin, D. (2003) 'The politics of policing: managerialism, modernization and performance', in R. Matthews and J. Young (eds), *The New Politics of Crime and Punishment*. Cullompton: Willan.

Martin, P.D., Schmitter, H. and Schneider, P.M. (2001) 'A brief history of the formation of DNA databses in forensic science within Europe', *Forensic Science International*, 119: 225–31.

Marx, G. (1988) *Undercover: Police Surveillance in America*. Berkeley, CA: University of California Press.

Marx, G.T. (2001) 'Technology and social control: the search for the illusive silver bullet', *The International Encyclopedia of the Social and Behavioral Sciences*.

Marx, G.T. (2002) 'What's new about the "New Surveillance"? Classifying for change and continuity', *Surveillance and Society*, 1 (1): 9–29

Matza, D. (1969) *Becoming Deviant*. Englewood Cliffs, NJ: Prentice Hall.

McCartney, C. (2003) 'The future of the National DNA Database', *The Magistrate*.

McCartney, C. (2006a) *Forensic Identification and Criminal Justice*. Cullompton: Willan.

McCartney, C. (2006b) 'Forensic DNA sampling and the England and Wales National Database: a sceptical approach', *Critical Criminology*, 12: 157–78.

McCartney, C. (2006c) 'The DNA expansion programme and criminal investigation', *British Journal of Criminology*, 46: 175–92.

McConville, M., Sanders, A. *et al.* (1991) *The Case for the Prosecution: Police Suspects and the Construction of Criminality.* London: Routledge and Kegan Paul.

McCulloch, H. (1996) *Police Use of Forensic Science.* London: Home Office Police Research Group.

McLaughlin, K. (2001) 'The permanent revolution: New Labour, new public management and the modernisation of criminal justice', *Criminal Justice*, 1: 301–18.

McLaughlin, K. (2002) *New Public Management: Current Trends and Future Prospects.* London: Routledge.

McLaughlin, C., Osborne, P. and Ferlie, E. (2001) *The New Public Management: Current Trends and Future Prospects.* London: Routledge and Kegan Paul.

Miller, P. and Rose, N. (1988) 'The Tavistock Programme: the government of subjectivity and social life', *Sociology*, 22: 171–92.

Morgan, J.B. (1990) *The Police Function and the Investigation of Crime.* Aldershot: Averbury.

Nakamura, Y., Leppert, M. *et al.* (1987) 'Variable number of tandem repeat (VNTR) markers for human gene mapping', *Science*, 235: 1616–22.

National Criminal Intelligence Service (2000) *The National Intelligence Model.* London: Home Office.

Nettleton, S. (1994) 'Inventing mouths: disciplinary power and dentistry', in C. Jones and R. Porter (eds) *Reassessing Foucault: Power, Medicine and the Body.* London: Routledge.

Netzel, L.R. (2003) 'The forensic laboratory', in S.H. James and J.J. Nordby (eds), *Forensic Science: An Introduction to Scientific and Investigative Techniques.* Boca Raton, FL: CRC Press, pp. 163–80.

Neyroud, P. (2003) 'Policing and Ethics', in T. Newburn (ed.), *Handbook of Policing.* Cullompton: Willan, pp. 578–602.

Nickell, J. and Fischer, J. (1999) *Crime Science: Methods of Forensic Detection.* Lexington: University of Kentucky Press.

Noaks, L., Levi, M. and Maguire, M. (eds) (1995) *Contemporary Issues in Criminology.* Cardiff: University of Wales Press.

Nobles, R. and Schiff, D. (2007) 'Misleading statistics in criminal trials', *Medicine, Science and the Law*, 47: 7–10.

Norris, C. and Armstrong, G. (1999) *The Maximum Surveillance Society: The Rise of CCTV.* Oxford: Berg.

Norris, C., Moran, J. and Armstrong, G. (eds) (1996) *Surveillance, Closed Circuit Television and Social Control.* Aldershot: Aldgate.

O'Malley, P. (1992) 'Risk, power and crime prevention', *Economy and Society*, 21: 252–75.

O'Neill, O. (2002) *Autonomy and Trust in Bioethics.* Cambridge: Cambridge University Press.

Osborne, D. and Gaebler, T. (1992) *Re-Inventing Government*. London: Addison-Wesley.

Packer, H. (1968) *The Limits of the Criminal Sanction*. Stanford, CA: Stanford University Press.

Pasquino, P. (1991) 'Criminology: the birth of a special knowledge', in G. Burchell, C. Gordon and P. Miller (eds), *The Foucault Effect: Studies in Governmentality*. Chicago: The University of Chicago Press.

Philips, D. (1985) '"A Just Measure of Crime, Authority, Hunters and Blue Locusts": the "revisionist" social history of crime and the law in Britain, 1750–1850', in S. Cohen and A. Scull (eds), *Social Control and The State*. Oxford: Blackwell, pp. 50–74.

Phillips, J. (1988) 'Practical advocacy – genetic fingerprinting', *The Australian Law Journal*, 67 (2): 550–52.

Pick, D. (1989) *Faces of Degeneration: A European Disorder*. Cambridge: Cambridge University Press.

R v Marper & S (2002a) EWHC 478 (Admin), High Court of Justice Queen's Bench Division Administrative Court.

R v Marper & S (2002b) EWCA Civ 1275. Court of Appeal (Civil Division).

R v Marper & S (2004) UKHL 39. House of Lords (Appellant Committee).

Rabinow, P. (1992) 'Galton's Regret: of types and individuals', in P.R. Billings (ed.), *DNA On Trial: Genetic Identification and Criminal Justice*. New York: Cold Spring Harbour Laboratory Press.

Rabinow, P. (1996) *Making PCR: A Story of Biotechnology*. Chicago: Chicago University Press.

Raine, J.W. and Willson, M.J. (1997) 'Beyond managerialism in criminal justice', *Howard Journal*, 36: 80–95.

Ratcliffe, J.H. (2002) 'Intelligence-led policing and the problems of turning rhetoric into practice', *Policing and Society*, 12: 52–66.

Redmayne, M. (2001) *Expert Evidence and Criminal Justice*. Oxford: Oxford University Press.

Reiner, R. (2000) 'Crime and control in Britain', *Sociology*, 34: 71–94.

Roberts, P. (1996) 'What price a free market in forensic science services?', *British Journal of Criminology*, 36: 37–60.

Roberts, P. and Willmore, C. (1993) 'The role of forensic science evidence in criminal proceedings', *Royal Commission on Criminal Justice Study*, 11. London: HMSO.

Roberts, P. and Zuckerman, A.A.S. (2004) *Criminal Evidence*. Oxford: Oxford University Press.

Robertson, B. and Vignaux, G.A. (1997) 'DNA on appeal', *New Zealand Law Journal*.

Robertson, G. (1992) 'The role of police surgeons', *The Royal Commission on Criminal Justice Research Study 6*. London: HMSO.

Roewer, L.M.K. *et al.* (2001) 'On Line Reference Database of European Y-chromosomal Short Tandem Repeat (STR) Haplotypes', *Forensic Science International*, 118: 106–13.

Rose, N. (1998) *Inventing Ourselves: Psychology, Power and Personhood.* Cambridge: Cambridge University Press.

Rose, N. (1999) *Powers of Freedom: Reframing Political Thought.* Cambridge: Cambridge University Press.

Rose, N. (2000) 'Government and control', *British Journal of Criminology*, 40: 321–39.

Rose, N. and Miller, P. (1992) 'Political power beyond the state: problematics of government', *British Journal of Sociology*, 43: 173–205.

Rothstein, M.A. (2005) 'Genetic justice', *New England Journal of Medicine*, 325: 2667–68.

Royal Commission on Criminal Justice (1993) *Cm 2263.* London: HMSO.

Sanders, A. and Young, R. (2002) 'From suspect to trial', in M. Maguire (ed.), *The Oxford Handbook of Criminology* (3rd edn). Oxford: Oxford University Press.

Sankar, P. (1997) 'Topics for our time: the proliferation and risks of government DNA databases', *American Journal of Public Health*, 87 (3): 336–37.

Sankar, P. (2001) 'DNA-Typing: Galton's eugenic dream realised?', in J. Caplan and J. Torpey (eds), *Documenting Individual Identity: The Development of State Practices in the Modern World.* Princeton: Princeton University Press.

Saulsbury, W., Hibberd, M. and Irving, B.L. (1994) *Using Physical Evidence: An Examination of Police Decision Making.* London: The Police Foundation.

Schneider, P.M. and Martin, P.D. (2001) 'Criminal DNA databases: the European situation', *Forensic Science International*, 119: 232–38.

Schultz, M.M. and Reichert, W. (2004) 'A strategy for STR analysis of cryptic epithelial cells on several textiles in practical casework', in G.F. Sensenbaugh, P.J. Lincoln and B. Olaisen (eds), *Progress in Forensic Genetics*, Vol. 8. Amsterdam: Elsevier, pp. 514–16.

Scottish Law Commission (1989) *Report on Evidence: Blood Group Tests, DNA Test and Related Matters.* Edinburgh: HMSO.

Sekula, A. (1986) 'The Body and the Archive', *October*, 39: 3–64.

Shriver, M., Frudakis, T. and Budowle, B. (2005) 'Getting the science and the ethics right in forensic genetics', *Nature Genetics*, 36: 449–50.

Sobrino, B., Brion, M. and Carracedo, A. (2005) 'SNPs in forensic genetics: a review on SNP typing methodologies', *Forensic Science International*, 154: 181–94.

Staley, K. and Wallace, H. (2004) *The Police National DNA Database: Balancing Crime Detection, Human Rights and Privacy.* Buxton: Genewatch.

Star, S.L. (1985) 'Work and uncertainty', *Social Studies of Science*, 15: 391–427.

Stenson, K. (1993) 'Community policing as a governmental technology', *Economy and Society*, 22: 373–99.

Steventon, B. (1993) *The Ability to Challenge DNA Evidence*. Royal Commission on Criminal Justice Research Study 9. London: HMSO.

Steventon, B. (1998) 'Statistical evidence and the courts – recent developments', *Journal of Criminal Law*, 62: 176–84.

Stewart, J. and Walsh. K. (1992) 'Change in the management of public services', *Public Administration*, 70: 499–518.

Strathern, M. (ed.) (2000) *Audit Cultures: Anthropological Studies in Accountability, Ethics and the Academy*. London: Routledge.

Sutherland, B. *et al.* (2002) 'Commentary on: Wickenhieser, R.A. Trace DNA: a review, discussion of theory, and application of the transfer of trace quantities of DNA through skin contact', *Journal of Forensic Sciences*, 47: 442–50.

Syndercombe-Court, D., Ballard, C., Phillips, A., Revoir, A., Robson, C. and Thacker, C. (2003), 'Comparison of Y chromosome haplotypes in three racial groups and the possibility of predicting ethnic origin', *International Congress of Serology*, 1239: 67–9.

Taylor, N. (2003) 'Policing, privacy and proportionality', *European Human Rights Law Review*, Special Issue.

Thompson, W.C. (1997) 'A sociological perspective on the science of forensic DNA testing', *University of California, Davis Law Review*, 30: 1112–36.

Thompson, W.C. and Schumann, E.L. (1987) 'Interpretation of statistical evidence in criminal trials: the prosecutor's fallacy and the defense attorney's fallacy', *Law and Human Behavior*, 11: 167–87.

Tilley, N. (2003) 'Community policing, problem-oriented policing and intelligence-led policing', in T. Newburn (ed.), *Handbook of Policing*. Cullompton: Willan, pp. 311–39.

Tilley, N. and Ford, A. (1996) *Forensic Science and Crime Investigation*. London: Home Office.

Touche Ross (1987) *Review of Scientific Support for the Police*. London: Home Office.

Townley, L. and Ede, R. (2004) *Forensic Practice in Criminal Cases*. London: The Law Society.

Tyler, M.G., Kirby, L.T. *et al.* (1986) 'Human blood stain identification and sex determination in dried blood stains using recombinant DNA techniques', *Forensic Science International*, 31: 267–72.

Tyler-Smith, C. (1999) 'Y-chromosomal DNA markers', in S.S. Papiha, R. Deka and R. Chakraborty (eds), *Genomic Diversity: Applications in Human Population Genetics*. New York: Plenum.

UKAS (2001) *Accreditation for Suppliers to the UK National DNA Database*. Feltham: United Kingdom Accreditation Service: 1–9.

Valier, C. (1998) 'True crime stories: scientific methods of criminal investigation, criminology and historiography', *British Journal of Criminology*, 38 (1).

Vallone, P.M. and Butler, J.M. (2004) 'Y-SNP typing of US African American and Caucasion samples using allele-specific hybridization and primer extension', *Journal of Forensic Sciences*, 49: 723–32.

van der Ploeg, I. (1999) 'The illegal body: 'Eurodac' and the politics of biometric identification', *Ethics and Information Technology*, 1: 295–302.

van der Ploeg, I. (nd) 'Biometrics, and the body as information: normative issues of the socio-technical coding of the body'. Unpublished manuscript.

van Hoofstdt, D.E.O. (1998) 'DNA fingerprinting and skin debris: sensitivity of capillary electrophoresis in forensic applications using PCR', *Second European Symposium on Human Identification*. Innsbruck, Austria: Promega Corporation.

van Oorschot, R.A.H. and Jones, M. (1997) 'DNA fingerprints from fingerprints', *Nature*, 387: 767.

van Oorschot, R.A.H., Weston, R.K. and Jones, M.K. (1998) 'Retrieval of DNA from touched objects', *Proceedings of the 14th Annual Symposium on the Forensic Sciences of Australia and New Zealand Forensic Science Society*, Adelaide, 12–16 October.

van Rentergeum, P. (2000) 'Use of latent fingerprints as a source of DNA for genetic identification', in G. Sensenbaugh (ed.), *Progress in Forensic Genetics*, Vol. 8. Amsterdam: Elsevier, pp. 501–03.

Wall, W. (2002) *Genetics and DNA Technology: Legal Aspects*. London: Cavendish Publishing.

Walsh, S.J. (2005) 'Legal perceptions of forensic DNA profiling: Part 1: a review of the legal literature', *Forensic Science International*, 155: 51–60.

Watanabe, Y. *et al.* (2003) 'DNA typing from cigarette butts', *Legal Medicine*, 5: 177–79.

Watson, N. (1999) 'The analysis of body fluids', in P. White (ed.), *Crime Scene to Court: The Essentials of Forensic Science*. Cambridge: The Royal Society of Chemistry, pp. 289–328.

Webb, B., Smith, C., Brock, A. and Townsley, M. (2005) 'DNA Fast-Tracking', in M.J. Smith and N. Tilley (eds), *Crime Science: New Approaches to Preventing and Detecting Crime*. Cullompton: Willan.

Werrett, D.J., and Sparkes, R. (1998) '300 matches per week: the effectiveness and future development of DNA intelligence databases', *Ninth International Symposium on Human Identification*. Wisconsin: Promega Corporation.

Wetton, J.H., Tsang, K.W. and Khan, H. (2005) 'Inferring the population of origin of DNA evidence within the UK by allele-specific hybridisation of Y-SNPs', *Forensic Science International*, 152: 45–54.

Wickenhieser, R.A. (2002) 'Trace DNA: a review, discussion of theory, and application of the transfer of trace quantities of DNA through skin contact', *Journal of Forensic Sciences*, 47: 442–50.

Wiegand, P. and Kleiber, M. (1997) 'DNA typing of epithelial cells after strangulation', *International Journal of Legal Medicine*, 110: 181–83.

Wiegand, P. and Kleiber, M. (1998) 'DNA typing of epithelial cells', in B.E.A. Olaisen (ed.), *Progress in Genetics*. Amsterdam: Elsevier, pp. 165–67.

Wiegand, P. *et al.* (1993) 'DNA typing of debris from fingernails', *International Journal of Legal Medicine*, 106: 81–3.

Wiegand, P. *et al.* (2000) 'STR typing of biological stains on strangulation tools', in G.F. Sensenbaugh, P.J. Lincoln and B. Olaisen (eds), *Progress in Forensic Genetics*, Vol. 8. Amsterdam: Elsevier.

Williams, R. and Johnson, P. (2004a) 'Circuits of surveillance', *Surveillance and Society*, 2 (1): 1–14.

Williams, R. and Johnson, P. (2004b) '"Wonderment and Dread": representations of DNA in ethical disputes about forensic DNA databases', *New Genetics and Society*, 23: 205–22.

Williams, R., Johnson, P. and Martin, P. (2004) *Genetic Information and Crime Investigation*. London: The Wellcome Trust.

Wyman, A.R. and White, R. (1980) 'A highly polymorphic locus in human DNA', *Proceedings of the National Academy of Science USA*, 77: 6754–58.

Y Chromosome Consortium (2002) 'A nomenclature system for tree of human Y chromosomal binary haplogroups', *Genome Research*, 12: 339–48.

Young, J. (1999) *The Exclusive Society: Social Exclusion, Crime and Difference in Late Modernity*. London: Sage.

Zifcak, S. (1994) *New Managerialism: Administrative Reform in Whitehall and Canberra*. Buckingham: Open University Press.

Index

Added to a page number 't' denotes a table and 'n' denotes notes.